Unlock Your Inner Child

A Simple, Powerful Path To Self Growth, Break Free From Childhood Trauma, Build Emotional Resilience & Reclaim Inner Strength

Summer Weston

OVER 75+
FREE COLOUR PRINTABLES

Enhance Your Inner Child Journey With These Digital Downloads - I have put together resources that I think will be useful for you while you are working through the book. Click the QR code below to get access.

Copyright © Summer Weston - All rights reserved.

The content contained within this book may not be reproduced, duplicated or transmitted without direct written permission from the author or the publisher.

Under no circumstances will any blame or legal responsibility be held against the publisher, or author, for any damages, reparation, or monetary loss due to the information contained within this book. Either directly or indirectly. You are responsible for your own choices, actions, and results.

Legal Notice:

This book is copyright protected. This book is only for personal use. You cannot amend, distribute, sell, use, quote or paraphrase any part, or the content within this book, without the consent of the author or publisher.

Disclaimer Notice:

Please note the information contained within this document is for educational and entertainment purposes only. All effort has been executed to present accurate, up to date, and reliable, complete information. No warranties of any kind are declared or implied. Readers acknowledge that the author is not engaging in the rendering of legal, financial, medical or professional advice. The content within this book has been derived from various sources. Please consult a licensed professional before attempting any techniques outlined in this book.

By reading this document, the reader agrees that under no circumstances is the author responsible for any losses, direct or indirect, which are incurred as a result of the use of the information contained within this document, including, but not limited to, — errors, omissions, or inaccuracies.

Contents

Introduction — VI

1. Chapter 1: Understanding Your Inner Child — 1
2. Chapter 2: Building Your Inner Strength — 17
3. Chapter 3: A Quiet Space to Find Yourself: Writing Your Way to Healing — 31
4. Chapter 4: Learning to Be Gentle with Yourself — 45
5. Chapter 5: Learning to Say No (And Mean It) — 57
6. Chapter 6: Healing Through Your Body — 71
7. Chapter 7: Growing Through the Hard Times & Putting Together Your Toolkit — 89
8. Chapter 8: Navigating Professional Life While Healing Your Inner Child — 95
9. Chapter 9: Your Healing Journey - Moving Forward with Courage and Hope — 105
10. References — 113

Introduction

The Key That Changed Everything

I was eight years old when I lost the front door key. Even now, decades later, I can feel that knot of panic in my stomach. It wasn't just about the key but about choosing between my parents. My Dad offered to help, his hand extended in a moment of unexpected kindness, but accepting meant betraying my Mum. You see, my Mum never actually said we couldn't talk to Dad, not through her words, but through the unspoken language of a bitter divorce. Every child of divorce knows this silent dialect of pain, this intricate dance of loyalty and survival.

That lost key became more than just a memory - it became a symbol of all the choices no child should have to make. Like many of you reading this, I grew up too fast. While other kids were playing with dolls or out playing with their friends, I was playing parent to my younger brother and sister, listening to the chaos of Mum's drunken fights with her boyfriends downstairs, trying to shield them from the screaming, all 3 of us sitting on the stairs crying. Sometimes, I even stood between Mum and her latest drunken boyfriend, a child trying to stop adult violence. How do you process that at eight or nine years old?

You might be nodding now if you were born between the early 60s and 90s. We come from a generation where feelings stayed buried, where 'therapy' was almost a dirty word, where you just got on with it. You may be carrying your own version of that lost key - a moment when childhood suddenly wasn't childhood anymore. But you're not alone. We share these experiences, and we can rebuild together.

I'm writing this book because of a moment that changed everything: that scared eight-year-old girl holding a lost key is still very much alive inside me. She's my inner child, and understanding her has been the most transformative journey of my life. For years, I was trapped in a cycle of toxic relationships, mistaking control for love and survival for connection. I was always trying to prove my worth, constantly feeling like I was never enough.

This isn't another dusty self-help book gathering cobwebs on a shelf. This is a lifeline, a conversation between two survivors, between me and you. I'm going to show you exactly how I broke free from the patterns that kept me stuck and how I learned to heal the wounds I'd been carrying since childhood. We'll walk through practical, real-world strategies for managing anxiety, setting boundaries that actually stick, and, most importantly, believing that you deserve good things.

If you've ever felt like you're constantly fighting an invisible battle, like you're carrying weight that isn't yours to carry, this book is for you. If you're tired of repeating the same painful patterns, of feeling like you're always bracing for the next blow—you're in the right place.

These are tools that work, and you have the power to use them.

Each chapter builds on the last, like stepping stones across a river. We'll use tools that work - journaling that doesn't feel forced, meditation that fits into real life, and exercises that help you understand why you react the way you do. You might be sceptical. You may have tried other books or approaches before. Perhaps you're thinking, 'My childhood wasn't that bad' or 'It's too late to change.' I felt that way too. But I promise you this: if I could transform my life from that scared little girl to someone who finally feels at peace with herself, so can you. This book is a promise and a roadmap to your healing and growth.

Ready to begin? I recommend that you use a journal or a notepad—anything where you can keep a note of what you discover. Let's take this journey together. Your inner child has been waiting for someone to finally listen.

Chapter 1: Understanding Your Inner Child

Do you remember feeling completely invisible as a child? One (of many) memories stands out crystal clear - standing at the school gates, watching other parents arrive to collect their children, knowing my Mum wouldn't be there. Not because she didn't care, but because by 3pm, she'd usually be several drinks in. I learned to get the bus home alone, clutching my bag and thinking what I might find when I got there. Would she be passed out on the sofa? Fighting with someone? That uncertainty became my normal.

One particularly vivid memory was finding her in a screaming match with one of our neighbours in the front garden, rolling around in the mud, pulling at each other's hair like teenagers. I can still feel that embarrassment and shame, wanting the ground to swallow me up as other kids crowded around to watch. This began a long journey of discovering the child within me—an integral part of who I am, shaped by memories, experiences, and emotions that I carried unknowingly into adulthood.

Your Inner Child: A Journey to Self-Discovery

Talking about your 'inner child' sounds a bit strange - maybe even a bit weird or woo-woo. But stay with me here. You know that feeling when something small triggers a huge reaction? Like when someone dismisses your idea in a meeting and suddenly you're that kid again, sitting in class afraid to raise your hand? Or when you see children playing freely in the park and something in you aches, remembering when you had to be the 'responsible one' way too young? That's your inner child speaking. Think of it this way - inside us, there's still that little person we used to be, holding onto both the magical moments and the hard stuff.

Sometimes, they show up unexpectedly - maybe in that flutter of excitement when you smell that freshly cooked Sunday roast your nan used to make or in that knot in your stomach when someone raises their voice, even if they're not angry at you.

One way to start understanding this part of yourself is through visualisation - a fancy word for simply closing your eyes and picturing yourself as a child. Don't worry; this isn't about getting lost in old memories or dwelling on the past. It's like finally sitting down and chatting with that younger version of you who's been trying to get your attention all these years. We'll explore some gentle ways to do this later in the book.

Nobody taught me how to understand my own pain. Survival was my only language—reading rooms, predicting emotions, and protecting those I loved. The skills that kept me safe then have followed me through decades of healing, like a map drawn in invisible ink.

Why Self-Discovery Matters

Healing isn't about erasing your past. It's about understanding how your experiences shaped you and recognizing the incredible strength that carried you through impossible moments. The wounds you carry are not weaknesses but evidence of your remarkable survival.

Let's 'Quiz' Your Inner Child

To help you discover more about your inner child, I have put together a list of questions, but not just any old questions. See them as an invitation, a gentle, brave conversation with the part of you that has carried so much for so long. Think of it as a mirror, not to judge, but to truly see yourself. Every blank space is an opportunity. Every reflection is a step toward healing. This questionnaire is designed to help you:

Recognise your survival strategies
Understand the emotional landscape of your childhood
Identify patterns that no longer serve you
Create compassionate awareness
Take the first step toward intentional healing

UNLOCK YOUR INNER CHILD

How to Use This Guide

There are no right or wrong answers. Some questions may be challenging. Others might unlock memories or emotions you've kept carefully hidden. That's okay. Move at your own pace. Take breaks when you need to. Treat yourself with the same gentleness you would offer a wounded child.

<u>Remember:</u> This is your journey. Your pace. Your healing. You might discover patterns you've never noticed before. Moments of clarity might surprise you. Some questions might bring tears. Others might spark unexpected hope. Each response is a piece of your healing puzzle.

A Word of Caution – If you find these questions triggering significant emotional distress, please:

Pause and take deep breaths
Reach out to a trusted friend or therapist
Remember that healing is not a linear process
Be kind to yourself

This questionnaire is not a diagnostic tool. It's a compassionate exploration—a chance to shine a gentle light on your inner world. It's your Invitation to turn the page when you're ready. There's no rush, no pressure, just an opportunity to meet yourself with radical compassion.

YOUR STORY MATTERS.

YOUR HEALING MATTERS.

YOU MATTER.

THERE ARE NO RIGHT OR WRONG ANSWERS—ONLY YOUR TRUTH.

Inner Child Self-Discovery Questionnaire

Childhood Landscape – Family Dynamics

1. Describe the emotional atmosphere of your childhood home in three

words:

2. Who was your primary caregiver?
☐ **Mother** ☐ **Father** ☐ **Grandparent** ☐ **Other**

3. As a child, did you feel:
Consistently safe
Sometimes anxious
Often afraid
Hypervigilant
Responsible for others' emotions

Emotional Patterns

4. Reflect on your earliest memory of feeling:
Loved
Scared
Alone

5. Complete this sentence in five different ways:
"As a child, I learned that love means..."

Survival Strategies – Coping Mechanisms

6. Check the survival strategies you recognise in yourself:
People-pleasing
Becoming invisible
Overachieving
Constant caretaking
Emotional numbing
Hypervigilance
Perfectionism
Other

7. Rate how these strategies show up in your current life (1-10 scale):
People-pleasing
Emotional guardedness
Need for control
Fear of conflict

Emotional Inheritance

8. Identify emotions you struggle to express:
Anger
Sadness
Vulnerability
Joy
Excitement
Disappointment
Other

9. Describe a situation where you felt emotionally overwhelmed as a child:

Relationship Patterns – Connection and Trust

10. In relationships, I tend to:
Push people away
Become overly attached
Maintain strict boundaries
Struggle with trust
Fear abandonment

11. My attachment style seems to be:
Secure
Anxious
Avoidant
Disorganized

12. When conflict arises, I typically:
Withdraw
Fight
Freeze
People-please
Analyse endlessly

Inner Child Dialogue – Deep Reflection

13. If I could speak to my younger self, I would say:
14. The part of my childhood I'm most healing from is:
15. Three words that describe my inner child:

Healing Intentions – Personal Growth

16. My biggest fear about healing is:
17. The most essential healing I need right now is:
Emotional
Relational
Professional
Spiritual
Physical
Other

18. Visualise your healed self. What feels different?

Reflection Guide

This questionnaire isn't about perfect answers but about gentle self-discovery. After completing:

Take a deep breath
Review your responses without judgment
Identify 2-3 patterns that surprise you
Choose one area to focus on in your healing journey

Recommended Next Steps:
Journal about your insights
Discuss with a trusted therapist
Practice self-compassion
Revisit this questionnaire every 6 months

Important Note: *This questionnaire is a tool for self-reflection, not a diagnostic instrument. If you experience significant emotional distress, please consult a mental health professional.*

What Happens If You Ignore Those Feelings

Over the years I have learned: that when we ignore these feelings from our past, they don't just go away. They're like those boxes in the attic we never unpack - they're still there, affecting everything from our anxiety levels to our relationships.

Maybe you find yourself constantly trying to please others, having difficulty trusting people, or feeling like you're never quite good enough. These patterns often start way back in childhood. That's why I've found journaling so helpful - and don't worry, I'm not talking about writing prize-winning essays here. Even just scribbling down thoughts in an old notebook can help. Any piece of paper will do. The important thing is just getting those thoughts out of your head and onto the page.

I get it - this might feel scary. I felt ridiculous the first time I tried connecting with my inner child. Part of me wanted to slam the book shut and go back to pretending everything was fine. That resistance is normal - it's your mind trying to protect you from old hurts. But here's the thing: something shifts when you show up with kindness for that younger version of yourself. You might find yourself being more patient with others, understanding your reactions better, and even healing relationships you thought were broken beyond repair. This isn't a quick fix or a one-time thing. Healing is like tending a garden - it takes time, patience, and regular care. Some days, you'll feel like you're making progress; others might feel like you're right back where you started. That's okay. What matters is that you're finally allowing yourself to acknowledge and care for all parts of you - especially that younger part waiting so long to be heard.

When Your Past Shows Up Uninvited

Ever notice how certain things seem to keep happening in your life? Like picking partners who somehow remind you of your chaotic childhood, even though that's precisely what you're trying to avoid? Or maybe you find yourself pushing away the good ones because a calm and loving relationship feels scarier than a dramatic one, even perhaps 'needing' to have the drama? That's not by chance - it's your past leaving fingerprints all over your present.

Trust is a big one. When I grew up, never knowing what to expect - whether my Mum would be passed out on the sofa or standing cooking dinner, appearing perfectly normal- it's no wonder trusting people feels like walking through a minefield. You want to believe people when they say they care, but there's always that voice in your head whispering, 'Just wait, they'll let you down too.'

Then there's anxiety - oh, the anxiety. You know those moments when your heart starts racing, your hands get sweaty, and maybe you're not even sure why? It's like your body remembers something your mind is trying to forget. Sometimes, it shows up as full-blown panic attacks;

sometimes, it's just this constant feeling of waiting for the other shoe to drop. Your body's still stuck in survival mode, always on high alert for the next disaster.

And let's talk about that voice in your head - the one that keeps telling you you're not good enough, not smart enough, not worthy enough. The one that has you apologising for breathing too loudly or taking up space. I bet sometimes you catch yourself saying sorry for things that aren't even your fault. That's not your voice - that's the echo of every time you were made to feel small, every time you had to be perfect to feel worthy of love.

I met somebody when I was around 21 – I thought he was *gorgeous!* Everything seemed great for 4 weeks and then it started, little comments at first, then causing arguments from nowhere, once leaving me in an area I had never been to before, on my own – the list goes on. But the biggest thing to this day 40 years later that I have never forgotten. He told me I was boring, really boring. In fact so boring that I made him yawn every time I spoke. For years afterward, I found myself apologising for every time somebody yawned in case I was boring them.

You might find yourself sabotaging good things before they can go wrong. Maybe you quit jobs just as you're about to get promoted or pick fights in relationships when everything's going too well. It's like there's a part of you that's more comfortable with chaos because at least that feels familiar.

Here's something you might recognise: You're at a family gathering, everything's fine, and then someone says something - maybe about how kids these days are too sensitive, or about how you should be grateful for your childhood because 'others had it worse.' Suddenly, your chest tightens up, your mind goes fuzzy, and you're right back there, feeling small and powerless. That's a trigger - it's your past raising its hand to remind you there's something that still needs healing.

The good news? Once you start spotting these patterns, you can start changing them.

TRY THIS:
TAKE A DEEP BREATH. FEEL YOUR FEET ON THE GROUND. REMIND YOURSELF THAT YOU'RE HERE, NOW, IN THIS MOMENT – NOT BACK THERE. YOU'RE SAFE, AND YOU GET TO CHOOSE HOW TO RESPOND.

Understanding all this isn't about pointing fingers or dwelling on the past. It's about finally connecting the dots between then and now. Once you see how these old wounds are still calling the shots in your life, you can start writing a new story where your past informs but doesn't control your future.

Learning to Listen: When Your Inner Child Speaks

Sometimes, just acknowledging these feelings can help them loosen their grip. It's like turning around and saying to that younger part of yourself, 'I hear you'. 'I get why you're scared/angry/sad'. And 'it makes total sense given what you went through.'

Understanding Your Reactions

Think about the last time something really got under your skin - maybe it was more significant than the situation seemed to deserve. Perhaps someone commented casually about your parenting, and you felt that familiar hot rush of shame and anger. Or maybe your partner was trying to help, but their suggestion made you feel small and defensive.

Try this:
Grab your notebook or journal (or even grab your phone), and let's break this down together:

What exactly happened? Just the facts, like you're describing a scene in a film

How did your body react? Maybe your chest got tight, or your stomach churned

What emotions came flooding in?

Did it remind you of anything from your past?

Here's a personal example: Someone told me I was 'too sensitive' about something a while ago. On the surface, it was just a throwaway comment. But suddenly, I was furious, with tears pricking at my eyes. When I took a moment to think about it, I realised I heard my mum's voice. All those times, she'd dismissed my feelings with 'Don't be so sensitive' or 'Don't be so silly' (we say that way too much to ourselves) when I was hurt or scared.

Have you ever snapped at someone you love over something tiny and thought, 'Whoa, where did that come from?' Or have you found yourself in a complete panic because someone's running late and hasn't texted? That's often your inner child trying to tell you something.

Think of your body and emotions like an alert system for your inner child. Sometimes, it's obvious - like that sick feeling in your stomach when someone raises their voice, even if they're not angry at you. Other times, it's more subtle - maybe you get a headache whenever you visit certain relatives, or your shoulders tense up during work meetings when someone talks over you. These aren't just random reactions - they're messages from that younger part of you still carrying around old hurts.

For example, Maybe you obsessively check your phone when a friend hasn't replied to your message. Your adult brain knows they're probably just busy, but there's this growing knot of anxiety in your chest. That might be your inner child remembering when you waited by the window for a parent who didn't show up or all those promised phone calls that never came.

Or perhaps you feel a flash of hurt and anger when you see friends posting photos of their happy family gatherings. While part of you feels guilty for these feelings (after all, you should be glad for them, right?), another part might be that little kid who always wished for a 'normal' family Christmas without arguments or drama.

Now I know that these feelings aren't wrong or silly - they're clues. They're like your inner child tugging at your sleeve, trying to show you something important. The trick is learning to pause when these big feelings show up. Try getting curious instead of pushing them away or beating yourself up about them. Ask yourself gently: 'What's really going on here? What part of me is feeling hurt right now?

How do you speak to yourself in these moments? Most of us have a harsh inner voice that says, 'You're overreacting again' or 'Why can't you just get over it?' But what if we tried something different?

Imagine talking to yourself like you'd talk to your best friend or a child you love. Instead of 'You're being ridiculous,' try 'Of course that upsets you - it makes perfect sense given what you've been through.' Instead of 'Get over it,' maybe 'It's okay to feel this way. Take all the time you need.'

This might feel weird at first - being kind to ourselves doesn't always come naturally, especially if we grew up having to be tough. But that younger part of you has been waiting a long time to hear these gentle words. You don't have to believe them entirely at first. Just try them on like you're testing out a new language.

Remember: Every time you catch yourself being harsh with yourself and choose a kinder response instead, you're healing not just your present self but that child within who needed to hear these words so long ago.

Unpacking Your Emotional Suitcase

Do you know that feeling when you're trying to pack for a trip and realise you're still wearing winter clothes in summer? Our emotional baggage works a bit like that - we're often lugging around stuff we don't need anymore, old hurts and fears that we picked up in childhood and never quite put down.

Think about it - maybe you freeze up when someone raises their voice, even in excitement. Or you may apologise twenty times a day for things that aren't even your fault. These aren't random habits - like old survival skills you learned when you were little. Back then, they kept you safe or helped you cope. But now? They might be weighing you down like trying to run with rocks in your pockets.

Something that blew my mind when I first realised it: Much of what we're carrying isn't ours. Maybe your Mum never learned to trust people because her Dad left when she was young. Then she taught you that people always leave without even meaning to. Or perhaps your Dad's family believed that showing emotions was weak, so he raised you to swallow your feelings, and now you struggle to tell people when you're hurting. We're all walking around with invisible suitcases packed full of 'shoulds' and 'shouldn'ts' that we inherited from our families. 'Don't cry.' 'Don't ask for help.' 'Don't trust anyone.' Sound familiar?

The tricky part is that these old patterns feel normal - as familiar as your reflection.   You may keep picking partners who need 'fixing' because taking care of others is what you've always done. Or you might push away anyone who shows you real love because you learned that you don't deserve it somewhere deep down. But here's the good news: once you start spotting these patterns, you can choose what to keep and let go of. It's like finally opening that suitcase and realising you no longer have to carry everything.

TRY THIS:
ONE OF THE MOST POWERFUL THINGS YOU CAN DO IS WRITE LETTERS - NOT TO SEND, JUST FOR YOU. WRITE TO THE PARENT WHO WASN'T THERE, THE FRIEND WHO BETRAYED YOU, OR EVEN YOUR YOUNGER SELF. POUR OUT ALL THE WORDS YOU NEVER GOT TO SAY. LET YOURSELF FEEL ANGRY, SAD, WHATEVER COMES UP. THIS ISN'T ABOUT FORGIVENESS (THOUGH THAT MIGHT COME LATER) - IT'S ABOUT FINALLY LETTING YOURSELF ACKNOWLEDGE HOW MUCH IT HURT.

Remember: You don't have to unpack everything at once. Take out one thing at a time, look at it, and decide if it still serves you. Some days, you might only manage to look at a tiny hurt, and that's okay. You're not just unpacking a weekend bag here - you're sorting through years of collected emotions. Give yourself time; give yourself grace.

'Is This Really Going to Help?'

Let's be honest - if you're feeling sceptical about all this inner child stuff, you're not alone. When I first heard about it, I thought it sounded like something from a cheesy self-help book. Looking back at your childhood? Talking to your younger self? It might seem a bit out there, especially if you're someone who prides themselves on being practical and getting on with things.

Maybe you're thinking, 'What's the point of digging up old stuff?' or 'Shouldn't I just focus on the future?' These are everyday thoughts. We live in a world big on 'tough it out' and 'get over it.' Most of us were raised to believe that looking back is weak and that we should push forward and stay strong. And let's face it - the idea of facing old hurts can be scary. It's like deciding whether to open that box in the attic that you know is full of memories you're not sure you want to revisit.

Now I have learned, from my own journey: THIS STUFF WORKS. Real people, just like you and me, have found their lives changing in ways they never expected.

I used to (and sometimes still do) instantly zoom in on what's wrong in every situation. Someone could do ninety-nine things right, but my brain would laser-focus on the one thing they did 'wrong.' It was exhausting - not just for others but for me too. Through this work, I started to see how this connected to my childhood, where I learned to be constantly on guard, always looking for what might go wrong next, because that felt safer than being caught off guard. When things were calm at home, it usually meant a storm was coming. So, I learned to spot the problems before they could surprise me. Understanding this pattern didn't make it vanish. Still, it helped me catch myself in those moments - to pause and ask, 'Am I really seeing the whole picture here, or am I just doing that old familiar thing of looking for what's wrong?'

I get it, though - starting this journey can feel overwhelming...

That's why we're going to take it slow. You don't have to dive into the deep end. Think of it more like dipping your toes in the water. Let's start with just 10 minutes a day - that's all. Use your special notebook or journal (nothing fancy, just something that's yours), and use it to jot down whatever comes to mind. Some days, you might write two lines, others two pages. There's no right or wrong way to do this. The goal isn't to live in the past or to blame anyone. It's more like being a detective in your own life, understanding why you react the way you do in certain situations.

Why do certain comments hit you so hard? Why do you always expect the worst? When you start connecting these dots, it's like turning on a light in a dark room - suddenly, things make more sense.

<u>Remember</u>: you're in control here. You decide how fast or slow to go. You choose what to explore and what to leave for another day. This isn't about ripping off all your emotional band-aids at once - it's about gentle understanding, one small step at a time.'

Why Does Childhood Leave Such Deep Footprints?

I learned something amazing that changed how I think about healing: Your brain is like a super-sophisticated recording device that never stops adapting. Even better? It can be rewired - yes, actually rewired - at any age. How incredible is that?

Let me break this down in a way that makes sense. Think about how a child learns to be careful around a hot stove - one touch, and their brain quickly writes a note: 'Hot stove = danger.' Well, our brains do the same thing with emotional experiences. When you grew up always having to spot what might go wrong (like me), your brain got really good at finding problems. It's like it created a super-highway for negative thoughts because that kept you safe back then. This is why sometimes we react before we even think - like when criticism sends us from zero to fury in seconds flat or when uncertainty makes our stomach churn. That's your brain's alarm system (scientists call it the amygdala) doing what it learned to do years ago. It's still running the same safety program it wrote when you were small, even though you're all grown up now.

But here's the good news - backed by proper science, not just feel-good stuff: your brain can learn new ways of responding. Remember how I mentioned rewiring? Scientists call this 'neuroplasticity' (fancy word, I know). It means your brain can create new pathways, like cutting new trails through a forest. You're making a new path every time you pause before reacting and choose to see the whole picture instead of just the problems.

_Think about this__:_ If your brain could adapt to protect you when you were little (even if those adaptations don't serve you anymore), it can also help you heal now. That's what makes the inner child work so powerfully - it's not just about thinking different thoughts; it's about actually reshaping how your brain processes experiences.

I was sceptical about all this at first. It sounded too simple - indeed if our brains were shaped by years of experience, we couldn't just change them now? But research shows that's exactly what we can do. You're building new neural connections every time you practice self-awareness and respond to yourself with understanding instead of criticism.

This isn't about erasing the past—it's about giving your brain new options for responding in the present. It's like having an old computer program that always defaults to 'look for danger' and slowly teaching it that other choices are available now.

♥ • ♥ • ♥ • ♥ • ♥

Chapter 1 Key Takeaways: Understanding Your Brain's Story

What We've Learned:

Your brain is incredibly adaptable - it can create new pathways and heal at any age.

Your automatic reactions (like always spotting problems first) aren't random - they're patterns your brain learned to keep you safe.

Childhood experiences shape how your brain responds to situations, but these responses can be rewired.
You're not stuck with old patterns - your brain can learn new, healthier ways of reacting.

Try These Steps This Week:

Notice Your Patterns

When you catch yourself focusing on what's wrong, pause
Ask yourself: 'Is this my old protective pattern showing up?'
Just notice - no judging or trying to change it yet

Start a Brain-Pattern Journal

Write down moments when you have strong reactions
Note what triggered you
Look for connections to your past

Remember:
You're gathering information, not criticising yourself

Practice Tiny Moments of Change

When you spot a problem, try to find one good thing too
Take three deep breaths before reacting
Remind yourself: 'That was then; this is now.'

Remember:
Change happens gradually
Your brain needs time to build new pathways
You don't have to do this perfectly
Every tiny moment of awareness is rewiring your brain
This work takes courage, and you're already showing it by being here

Chapter 2: Building Your Inner Strength

You know those people who seem to glide through life's storms while the rest of us feel like we're being tossed around in a hurricane? For years, I used to wonder what their secret was. What did they have that I didn't? It turns out that it wasn't some magical gift they were born with - it was something called emotional resilience. Think of it like building emotional muscles. Just like you can train your body to become stronger, you can actually train your mind to handle life's ups and downs better.

It's not about being unbreakable or never feeling hurt. It's about learning how to bend instead of break when life gets rough. And trust me, if someone who used to crumble at the first sign of trouble can understand this (yes, that's me), anyone can.

One of my biggest game-changers was learning to look at things differently. You know how when you're driving and stuck in traffic, you can either sit there getting increasingly frustrated or use the time to listen to your favorite podcast? It's the same situation, but it's an entirely different experience. That's what we call 'reframing'—finding a different way to look at what's happening to us.

The people we surround ourselves with make a massive difference, too. Ever notice how being around someone who's always complaining can make everything feel ten times worse? It's like their negativity has its own gravity, pulling you down with it. But spend time with someone who faces life's challenges with courage and hope, and suddenly, you feel stronger, too. Their strength somehow rubs off on you.

Managing everyday stress is crucial, too. I'm not talking about anything fancy—sometimes, it's as simple as taking three deep breaths when you feel overwhelmed or going for a walk when your thoughts start spiraling. It's about finding what works to stay steady when things get wobbly.

The beautiful thing about building resilience is that it changes everything.

Those situations that used to feel like the end of the world? They start feeling more like bumps in the road. That voice in your head that used to say, 'I can't handle this'? It starts saying, 'I've got this' instead—not all at once, mind you—but bit by bit, day by day.

Try This: Want to start building your own resilience? Let's start with something simple — grab your journal (or any piece of paper will do). Try writing about a challenge you're facing right now. But here's the twist — after you write about what's hard, write about what this situation might teach you. What strengths are you developing because of it? How might this make you stronger in the future?

Understanding Emotional Strength

Building emotional strength is a journey that lasts our whole life. It helps us cope better when times are tough and creates space for healing and growth. It isn't about never feeling pain or avoiding difficult emotions; it's about developing the capacity to

Experience emotions fully
Learning to process feelings without being overwhelmed
Creating internal stability during life's challenges
Building a compassionate relationship with yourself

The tools and tips we"ll explore together will help you build this strength so your past experiences don't have to control your present life.

Understanding Mindfulness: A Simple Way to Stay Present

Think of mindfulness as simply paying attention to what's happening right now. It's like pressing a pause button on your busy thoughts to notice how you're feeling now. While some people think mindfulness means you have to meditate in a quiet room, that's not true! You can practice mindfulness anywhere – while walking, eating, or even washing dishes.
Why does this matter for healing? Mindfulness helps us better handle difficult emotions and memories. Instead of getting swept away by thoughts about the past, we can anchor ourselves in the present moment, which helps us feel calmer and more in control.

Getting Started with Mindfulness

Here are two simple ways to begin:

Breathing Practice: Take a moment to notice your breath. Feel how it moves in and out of your body. Whenever your mind wanders (which is totally normal!), gently bring your attention back to your breathing. You can do this while sitting in traffic, standing in line at the store, or anytime you need a moment of calm.

Body Check-In: Take a few minutes to notice how your body feels, starting from your toes and moving up to your head. Where do you feel tense? Where do you feel relaxed? This helps you understand what your body tells you and can help you release stress.

When you practice mindfulness, you're learning to watch your thoughts and feelings without getting caught up in them. Think of it like watching clouds pass in the sky – you can see them without chasing after them. Practise being fully present, pay attention to the sensory experiences of the moment, and be in that moment! Whether you are washing the dishes, walking, or eating, you can practice this. Feel the texture of the soap suds, hear and feel the rhythm of your footsteps, and know what your food smells and tastes like.

These simple, easy acts of mindfulness are surprisingly easy to incorporate into your day and help you stay grounded and centred. I practise this myself when out walking, challenging myself to see several things I have never noticed before during the same walk.

Now, let's explore some guided exercises to incorporate mindfulness into your routine.

Mindful eating is a practice that transforms a simple meal into a different experience. Start by taking a moment to really appreciate the colors and smell of your food—how many of the individual ingredients can you actually taste? As you take each bite, savour the flavors and textures, chewing slowly and mindfully. Notice the sensations in your mouth and the feeling of nourishment. This practice will improve your appreciation for food, and double whammy: It's good for digestion!

Walking meditation is another technique that blends movement with

mindfulness. As you walk, really focus on the sensation of your feet touching the ground. Hear your steps beneath you, feel the weight shift with each step, move your legs, and breathe rhythmically. This practice can be done anywhere, whether in nature or in your living room.
By building mindfulness into everyday activities, you create a continuous thread of awareness that supports your healing process.

Your Turn to Reflect

Take a moment to think about when your feelings or thoughts felt too big to handle. Maybe your mind was racing, or your emotions felt overwhelming. What happened? How did it feel in your body?
Imagine you had a pause button—a way to step back and notice these feelings without being swept away by them. Mindfulness can offer this.

TRY THIS: WRITE DOWN YOUR EXPERIENCE AND ASK YOURSELF: WHAT WAS GOING THROUGH MY MIND AT THAT TIME? HOW MIGHT TAKING A FEW MINDFUL BREATHS HAVE HELPED? WHAT WOULD IT FEEL LIKE TO WATCH THESE THOUGHTS FLOAT BY INSTEAD OF GETTING CAUGHT UP IN THEM?

Remember: The goal isn't to make your thoughts go away. We're not trying to empty our minds or become super-peaceful monks! Instead, think of mindfulness as making friends with your thoughts and feelings. It's about watching them with kindness like you would watch clouds passing in the sky. Mindfulness becomes your personal anchor with practice – something you can hold onto when life feels stormy.

Finding Your Calm: Simple Ways to Ground Yourself

Do you ever feel like your mind is racing away with worrying thoughts? Grounding is like having a magic reset button for those moments. It's a simple way to bring yourself back to the here and now when you're feeling overwhelmed.

THINK OF IT THIS WAY: WHEN YOUR THOUGHTS ARE SPINNING LIKE A MERRY-GO-ROUND GOING TOO FAST, GROUNDING HELPS YOU STEP OFF AND FIND SOLID GROUND AGAIN. IT'S NOT COMPLICATED – ANYONE CAN DO IT, AND IT CAN HELP YOU FEEL BETTER IMMEDIATELY.

Let's explore some easy ways to ground yourself:

Using Your Senses: Your five senses are like anchors that can keep you steady when you're feeling wobbly:

Run your hands under warm water and notice how it feels

Hold something with an interesting texture, like a smooth stone or a fuzzy sweater

Look around and name five things you can see right now

Creating a Safe Place in Your Mind:

Sometimes, we need a mental escape hatch when things feel too much. Try picturing your own peaceful place. It could even be a sunny garden filled with flowers or maybe it's a quiet beach where you can hear gentle waves. You can visit this special place in your mind whenever you need a moment of calm. The best thing about grounding is that you can do it anywhere. It's like having a personal calm-down kit you always carry.

Positive Affirmations: Planting Seeds of Self-Love

Think of positive affirmations as gentle reminders you give yourself - like leaving kind little notes from a friend on your mirror. When you repeat words like 'I am worthy' or 'I am growing stronger every day,' you're actually helping rewire how your brain thinks about yourself. Your subconscious listens and believes everything that you say. When you are speaking to yourself badly, it listens (and believes you).

Try doing something different - It might feel a bit strange at first, like you're just saying empty words. But imagine you're watering a garden - each time you speak these encouraging words to yourself, you're nurturing new, healthier thoughts to grow. Over time, these affirmations can help quiet that harsh inner critic we all carry around and replace doubtful thoughts with more supportive ones. The best part is that you can practice affirmations anywhere - while brushing your teeth, during your morning coffee, or even stuck in traffic. They're beneficial when you're having a tough day or feeling those old wounds from your past creeping up. By choosing words that really matter to you and repeating them regularly, you're giving yourself a powerful tool for healing and growth.

*IF YOU WOULD LIKE A FREE LIST OF POSITIVE AFFIRMATIONS IN ADDITION TO THE ONES IN THIS BOOK, I HAVE PUT TOGETHER A SET OF DIGITAL FLASHCARDS. YOU WILL FIND A QR CODE AT THE BEGINNING OF THIS BOOK THAT CONTAINS A LINK FOR YOU TO DOWNLOAD THEM.

Healing Affirmations: Love Notes to Your Inner Child

Just like a child needs to hear 'I love you' and 'you're doing great,' your inner child needs these gentle reminders, too. Let's look at affirmations that can comfort and support your younger self.

When you feel small or scared, say, 'I am safe now, and I protect myself with love.' It is like giving your younger self a warm, cosy security blanket. Your adult self is now the protector you might have needed back then.

If you're dealing with old feelings of not being good enough, say, 'I was always worthy of love, even when I didn't know it.' This is like reaching back in time and hugging that younger version of you who might have doubted their worth.

For times when you're being hard on yourself about mistakes, try 'I'm learning and growing every day, just like I was meant to.' Remember how children naturally learn through trial and error? You're still allowed to learn that way, too.

When old pain surfaces, acknowledge it with, 'I hear you, I see you, and your feelings matter.' Sometimes, your inner child needs to know it's being listened to, like when a friend sits with you through a challenging moment.

Here are some more healing affirmations you might connect with:

'The child in me deserves all the patience and kindness in the world.'

'I embrace both my strength and sensitivity - they make me whole.'

'It's okay to take up space and let my voice be heard.'

'I choose to parent myself with gentleness and understanding.'

Remember, these words might initially feel big or strange - that's completely normal. Try them on like you would a new piece of clothing. Some might feel just right, while others might need adjusting. You can change the words to make them feel more authentic to you. The most powerful affirmations are the ones that make your heart feel a little lighter when you say them.

Start with just one that really speaks to you. Write it on your phone or put it somewhere you'll see it each morning. Let it be your gentle companion throughout the day, especially when your inner child feels scared or unsure. Over time, you might notice these words becoming less like something you're just saying and more like something you truly believe - like a flower slowly opening its petals to the sun.

Simple Ways to Feel Calmer Right Now

Think of grounding as dropping an anchor when your mind feels stormy. It's like pressing a gentle pause button on racing thoughts and returning to the here and now. The best part? The more you practice this, the better you stay steady when life gets wobbly.

TRY THIS: HERE'S A SUPER SIMPLE WAY TO START — IT'S CALLED THE 5-4-3-2-1 GAME, AND YOU CAN PLAY IT ANYWHERE, ANYTIME. IT'S LIKE GOING ON A LITTLE TREASURE HUNT WITH YOUR SENSES:

Find 5 things you can see (maybe the blue mug on your desk or the way sunlight hits the wall)

Touch 4 different things (feel the soft fabric of your shirt or the smooth surface of a table)

Listen for 3 different sounds (birds outside, the hum of your fridge, your own breath)

Notice 2 things you can smell (maybe your morning coffee or fresh air)

Find 1 thing you can taste (even just noticing the taste in your mouth counts)

TRY THIS: ANOTHER LOVELY WAY TO GROUND YOURSELF IS TO CREATE A SAFE PLACE IN YOUR MIND — LIKE HAVING A SECRET GARDEN YOU CAN VISIT WHENEVER YOU NEED TO. CLOSE YOUR EYES AND PICTURE SOMEWHERE THAT MAKES YOU FEEL COMPLETELY SAFE AND COSY. IT COULD BE A REAL PLACE, LIKE YOUR GRANDMOTHER'S KITCHEN, OR SOMEWHERE MAGICAL YOU MAKE UP, LIKE A CLOUD HOUSE IN THE SKY.

MAKE IT YOURS BY FILLING IT WITH EVERYTHING THAT MAKES YOU FEEL GOOD — MAYBE SOFT BLANKETS, WARM LIGHTS, OR THE SOUND OF GENTLE WAVES.

The beautiful thing about learning these techniques is that they're like having a trusty umbrella—always there when you need it. You're not trying to push away your feelings (they're all welcome here!) but instead creating a calm, steady space where you can feel them safely. Think of it as building your own emotional safety net, one practice at a time.
It might initially feel wobbly, like learning to ride a bike. That's totally okay! With time, reaching for these grounding tools will become as natural as reaching for your favourite comfort sweater when cold. Whether you're stuck in a busy shopping mall or lying awake at night with a buzzing mind, these techniques are your faithful friends, always ready to help you find your way back to solid ground.

Picturing Your Future Self: A Path to Healing

Have you ever been aware of how your mind can make your heart race just by thinking about something scary? We can use that same power of imagination to help us heal. It's like test-driving your future self—giving yourself a sneak peek at who you're becoming.

TRY THIS: CLOSE YOUR EYES FOR A MOMENT. WHAT WOULD IT FEEL LIKE TO WAKE UP ONE MORNING AND FIND THAT THE HEAVY BACKPACK OF PAST HURTS FEELS LIGHTER? MAYBE YOU SEE YOURSELF LAUGHING EASILY WITH FRIENDS, STANDING TALL IN MEETINGS, OR FINALLY FEELING AT PEACE WHEN YOU'RE ALONE WITH YOUR THOUGHTS. THE MORE ACCURATE YOU MAKE THIS PICTURE IN YOUR MIND, THE MORE IT FEELS POSSIBLE.

You might wonder, 'Is this just playing pretend?' Not at all! Athletes always do this - they run through their perfect performance in their minds before they step onto the field. Your brain doesn't know the difference between what you're imagining and what's happening. You have to admit, that's pretty amazing, right?

TRY THIS: FIND A QUIET MOMENT IN YOUR DAY — MAYBE WHEN YOU WAKE UP OR JUST BEFORE BED. PICTURE YOURSELF AS IF YOU'RE WATCHING A MOVIE, BUT YOU'RE THE STAR. HOW DO YOU

WALK? WHAT'S YOUR SMILE LIKE? HOW DO YOU HANDLE THOSE TRICKY SITUATIONS THAT THROW YOU OFF BALANCE? REALLY LET YOURSELF FEEL THE CONFIDENCE IN YOUR STEPS, THE WARMTH IN YOUR CHEST, AND THE CALM IN YOUR MIND.

The more you practice this, even just a few minutes daily, the more natural it feels. It's like trying on clothes that feel too fancy initially, but after wearing them a few times, you realise they fit you perfectly. Your mind begins thinking, 'Hey, maybe this is who I am.' Remember, you're not pretending these changes have already happened - you're showing your brain what's possible, like drawing a map for a journey you're ready to take. Whenever you picture your stronger, happier self, you're laying down stepping stones toward becoming that person.

Making Your Dreams Feel Real: Small Steps to Big Changes

You know that feeling when you're looking forward to something - maybe a holiday - and you can't stop thinking about it? Your whole body gets excited, and suddenly, packing your suitcase doesn't feel like such a chore. That's the magic of visualisation at work! When we picture good things ahead, our minds and bodies team up to help make them happen.

Let me share a story about Sarah. She used to wake up every morning feeling stuck, as if she was wearing shoes that were two sizes too small. Life had taught her to make herself small and doubt her voice. But she started doing something that seemed so simple that it was almost silly at first; she began spending five minutes each morning imagining herself standing tall, speaking up in meetings, and laughing freely with friends who really understood her. At first, it felt like she was playing pretend. But then something interesting started happening. One day, when her partner made a cutting remark about her ideas (something that usually made her shrink), she heard that confident version of herself she'd been picturing speak up instead. It wasn't dramatic - she said, 'I don't agree with that.' But it was huge for her. That small moment of courage led to bigger ones. Little by little, she started making choices that matched the person she saw in her mind - the one who knew she deserved good things. She found the strength to leave the relationship that was dimming her light. She applied for jobs she would've talked herself out of before. She started spending time with people who made her feel like her best self.

Think of visualisation like test-driving your future self. You could picture yourself taking three deep breaths instead of snapping when someone pushes your buttons. Or perhaps you see yourself saying 'no' to things that drain you without feeling guilty. The more you run through these scenes in your mind, the more natural they feel when it's showtime in real life.

Footballers do this all the time - before a big game, they'll play it out in their minds, seeing themselves making that perfect shot and scoring that winning goal. They're not just daydreaming; they're teaching their minds and bodies what success feels like. And you can do the same thing with your healing journey. Just like you're not the person you were five years ago, the future you picture for yourself might change too - and that's not only okay, it's healthy! Some days, you might see yourself confidently leading a team meeting; other days, you might picture yourself finding peace in quiet moments alone. Let your mind wander to what feels right for you right now.

Creating Your Cosy Corner: A Place Just for You

Everyone needs a spot to be themselves - no pretending, no masks, just you. Think of it as your own little hideaway from the world's noise. It doesn't have to be anything fancy or big. It could be a corner of your bedroom with your favorite throw or blanket, a cup of tea, or a special chair by the window where you can watch the world go by. Having this space is like having your own private recharging station. It's where you can take off the armour you might wear all day and breathe. Maybe you've noticed how different you feel when you step into a place that feels completely safe - your shoulders drop, your breathing slows down, and that knot in your stomach loosens a bit.

Your special spot might have things that make you feel good - soft pillows, calming colours, pictures that make you smile, or a plant that reminds you of growth and new beginnings. Some people like to keep a journal here; others might have their favourite books or music nearby. Getting the lighting right plays a massive part in creating the right ambience. Choosing soft lighting to create a soothing environment, or candles or fairy lights add a touch of magic and tranquility. But what matters is that this space feels right for you. This isn't just about having a nice place to sit - it's about giving yourself permission to have boundaries, to take time for yourself, and to honour your need for peace and quiet. Knowing you have this space to return to can feel like having a safety net when the world feels too loud or your thoughts are racing.

Making Your Space Work for You

What you do in your special place can become like daily promises to yourself. You could start each morning with five minutes of quiet breathing or end your day writing down your thoughts. These small routines might seem simple, but they're like building blocks, helping you feel more steady when life gets wobbly. Your space can change with you, too. Sometimes, you need a quiet corner for thinking, and other times, a spot to stretch or move your body. It's okay to switch things up—your needs might be different from one day to the next. Adding little touches that speak to your heart can make your space feel even more like home. There may be a photo that always makes you smile or a small treasure from a happy memory. Some people find that certain scents help them relax - like the smell of vanilla candles or fresh lavender. It's whatever works for you - there's no rule book here. This is your place to let your guard down and be exactly who you are now. It's okay to cry here, laugh, sit in silence, or dance - whatever feels right. Think of it as your private garden where you can tend to your inner self. Some days, you might feel like pulling out weeds (those old thoughts that don't serve you anymore); others, you might want to sit and watch things grow.

Remember, healing isn't a race to some finish line - it's more like tending to a constantly growing and changing garden. Having this special place is your way of saying 'I matter' and 'My peace matters.' It's a gift you give yourself, a reminder that you deserve a space in this world that feels completely and totally yours.

Taking Off the Mask: Finding Strength in Being Real

You know that feeling when you're wearing clothes that aren't quite 'you'? It could be an outfit that looks good but doesn't feel right. Many of us wear emotional outfits that don't fit - trying to be tough when we feel soft inside or acting like everything's fine when it isn't. But here's the thing: real strength isn't about keeping those masks on - it's about having the courage to take them off.

Being vulnerable might sound scary. After all, most of us learned early on to protect our hearts, like building a fort around our feelings. But think of vulnerability more like opening a window in a stuffy room - yes, it might feel a bit uncomfortable at first, but that fresh air is the very thing we need to breathe freely again. Finding safe people to be honest with is like finding the right soil to plant seeds in. These people won't judge you for having feelings, won't use your vulnerable moments against you, and make you feel like it's okay to be exactly who you are. Sometimes, it's a friend, a family member, or a therapist—someone who can hold space for your truth. When we dare to be vulnerable, something magical happens in our relationships. It's like opening a door and inviting others to step closer. Suddenly, conversations go deeper than just talking about the weather or what's on TV. Even during disagreements, being honest about how we feel (instead of just getting angry) can turn arguments into moments of fundamental understanding.

Remember: vulnerability isn't about spilling your life story to everyone you meet. It's about choosing moments to be your authentic self, to let down your guard with people who've earned your trust. It's about saying, 'This is me' - not perfect, not consistently strong, but perfectly human.

Your vulnerability is like a superpower in disguise. It's the key to unlocking deeper connections, genuine relationships, and true healing. When you allow yourself to be seen—really seen—you give others permission to do the same. And in that sharing, we all become a little more whole.

Chapter 2 Key Takeaways: Opening Your Heart to Heal

What We've Learned:

Being vulnerable isn't a weakness - it's actually one of the bravest things you can do
Those protective walls we built as children might have kept us safe then, but they might be holding us back now
Everyone carries emotional baggage - recognising what's in yours is the first step to setting it down
Your brain has a fantastic ability to create new patterns and heal old wounds
Building inner strength happens one small step at a time

Try These Steps This Week:

Start Noticing Your Patterns.
When do you put your walls up?
What situations make you feel defensive?
What old stories do you tell yourself in challenging moments? Just notice them - no judging, no trying to change yet.

Practice Small Moments of Trust

Share one honest feeling with someone you trust.
Let someone help you with something small.
Notice when you want to hide and ask yourself why?

Begin Your Healing Routine

Set aside 10 minutes each day for yourself.
Find a quiet space where you feel safe.
Start your journal - remember, no one else needs to see it.
Write down one thing you're proud of each day.

Remember:
Healing isn't linear - some days will feel more manageable than others.

You get to go at your own pace.
Small steps forward are still steps forward.
You're not alone in this journey.

Looking Ahead: In the next chapter, we'll explore specific tools and techniques for working with your inner child. Keep your journal handy—we'll be using it more as we explore this work further.

Chapter 3: A Quiet Space to Find Yourself: Writing Your Way to Healing

I felt silly the first time I wrote about my feelings. What was I supposed to say? But once I started, it was like finding a key to a door I didn't even know was locked. Just me, a notebook, and all these thoughts I'd been carrying around finally had somewhere to go.

Writing down your thoughts isn't about creating perfect prose - it's more like having an honest chat with yourself. Sometimes, you might surprise yourself with what comes out on the paper. That's the magic - you start writing about one thing, and suddenly, you're understanding feelings you didn't even know you had. Making journaling part of your day is like making a coffee date with yourself. You may be a morning person who likes to write while the world is still quiet, or you prefer unwinding with your journal before bed. What matters is finding a time that feels right for you and trying to stick with it. Think of it as setting aside a few minutes to check in with yourself, just like you would with a good friend.

There are many ways to journal, and none are wrong. Sometimes, let your thoughts flow, writing whatever pops into your head without worrying if it makes sense - like cleaning out a cluttered drawer where you need to pull everything out to see what's there. Other times, you may want more direction. Try answering questions like 'What made me smile today?' or 'What's something I wish I could tell someone?' Some people like to keep a gratitude journal, jotting down the good stuff in their day, even on the tough days when you have to look a bit harder to find it.
The important thing is finding a way that feels natural to you. That could mean writing in short bursts, or you prefer longer sessions where you can really dive deep. Some days, you might write pages, others just a few lines - and that's perfectly okay.

Gentle Exploration Of A Feeling

Here's a gentle way to start exploring your feelings through writing. Think of it as dipping your toes in the water rather than diving straight in. Pick a recent moment when you felt something strongly - anything from burst-out-loud happiness to that heavy feeling in your chest when something upset you. Maybe it was the joy of an unexpected call from an old friend or the frustration of being stuck in traffic when you were already running late. Take your pen and paper (or open your notes app - whatever feels right), and try answering these questions in your own way:

What was happening around you when this feeling showed up?

Where did you feel it in your body? Maybe your shoulders got tight, or your stomach felt fluttery

If this feeling could talk, what would it be trying to tell you?

Don't worry about writing perfectly or making it sound good - this is just for you. Sometimes, our feelings are trying to tell us something important, like when anger might actually be saying, 'Hey, someone crossed your boundaries,' or excitement about a new project might point you toward something you care about. You might notice patterns starting to emerge as you write—like feeling most alive when creating something, or you may see certain situations always leave you feeling drained. These little discoveries are gold—like clues that help you better understand yourself. This is your space, to be completely honest. No one else needs to see what you write, so you can say exactly what you feel without worrying about how it sounds or what anyone else might think.

Journal Prompts That Open Your Heart

Here are some prompts that can help you dig deeper into understanding yourself. Remember, there's no pressure to write pages - even a few honest sentences can unlock new insights.

Looking Back with Kindness

Think about writing a letter to your younger self at a specific age. What do they need to hear right now?
Think about a moment when you felt really proud of yourself. What made

that moment special?
Remember a time when you felt hurt. What would you say to that version of yourself now?

Understanding Your Present

What makes you feel truly safe? It might be a place, a person, or even a tiny ritual
What do you need more of in your life right now? Less of?
What's something you've been holding onto that you're ready to release?

Exploring Your Feelings

When was the last time you felt your authentic self? What was happening?
What makes you feel strong?
When do you feel most vulnerable?
If your emotions could speak directly to you today, what would they say?

Looking at Relationships

Think of someone who makes you feel good about yourself.
What is it about them that does this?
What boundaries do you wish you could set but haven't yet?
Who do you find it easiest to be yourself around? What makes it easy?

Dreams and Hopes

If you knew you couldn't fail, what would you try?
What small change could you make today that your future self would thank you for?
What does healing look like to you?
How will you know when you're making progress?

Daily Check-Ins

What's one thing that made you smile today?
Where did you notice tension in your body today?
What was happening when you noticed it?
What's something you did today that was just for you?

Remember, you can always come back to these prompts another day or use them as starting points and let your writing take you somewhere else entirely. The goal isn't to answer them all - it's to start a conversation with yourself.

Questions That Open Doors

Sometimes, the most powerful questions are the simplest ones. Do you know those moments when someone asks you something, and suddenly, you see your whole life differently? That's what we're aiming for here—but instead of waiting for someone else to ask, we will learn how to ask ourselves these game-changing questions.
Think of these reflection prompts as having a heart-to-heart with yourself—not the kind where you beat yourself up about past mistakes, but the kind where you sit down with a cup of tea and really listen to what's going on inside. These questions are your flashlight in a dark room—they help you see things that have always been there, just waiting to be discovered.

Let's start with something that might seem simple:

Here are some questions that might open up new ways of understanding yourself. Take your time with these - maybe pick just one to sit with for a few days:

1. **'What makes me feel strong?'** Think about times when you've felt really capable and solid in yourself. It might not be what you expect - sometimes, our real strength shows up in quiet moments, like when we choose to walk away from drama or ask for help even though it's hard.

2. **'When do I feel most like myself?'** Is it when you're alone? With certain people? Doing something specific? Notice the situation and how your body feels in these moments - are your shoulders relaxed? Is your breathing easier?

3. **'What would I try if I knew no one would judge me?'** This isn't about wild adventures (unless that's your thing). Maybe it's about wearing bright colours when you usually stick to black or saying no to things you usually feel obligated to do.

4. **'What patterns am I repeating from my childhood?'** Look at your reactions to stress - do you hide away like you did in your

room as a kid? Do you try to fix everything like you had to do for your family? Just notice these patterns with kindness.

5. **'What do I need right now that I'm not letting myself have?'** This could be something simple like rest or bigger things like asking for support. Often, we deny our basic needs because we learned somewhere along the way that we weren't supposed to have them.

6. **'What did I need to hear as a child that I still need to hear today?'**

Remember, there's no pressure to answer all of these at once. You should write about one in your journal or let it roll around in your mind while doing other things. These questions are like seeds - some might sprout right away, others might need more time. Also, you don't need to set aside hours for this—even five minutes before bed or while having your morning coffee can be enough.

Some people like to write their answers down (remember that journal we talked about?), while others prefer to think about them while taking a walk. There's no right or wrong way to do this. The first answer that pops into your head isn't always the whole story. Maybe when you ask yourself what makes you happy, your first thought is 'success' or 'having enough money.' But if you sit with that question a little longer, you might find other answers bubbling up - like the peace you feel when you're creating something or the warmth of spending time with someone who really gets you.

The beauty of these questions is that they grow with you. Ask yourself the same question next month or year, and you might get completely different answers. That's not because the first answers were wrong - it's because you're growing, changing, understanding yourself better.

Remember, there are no 'right' answers here. If a question doesn't speak to you right now, that's okay. It may not be the right time for that question, or you may ask it differently. The goal isn't to force insights but to create space for them to emerge naturally.

Checking In With Yourself: How Do You Know You're Healing?

Are you actually making progress? Sometimes, healing can feel like watching grass grow—you're unsure if anything changes until you look back and realise how far you've come. That's why checking in with yourself regularly, like taking snapshots of where you are on your journey, is helpful. Now, I'm not talking about grading yourself or beating yourself up about 'not doing well enough.' Think of it more like checking a map on a long road trip - you're just getting your bearings. Where are you now? What's feeling better? What still needs some tender care? Finding a quiet moment for these check-ins is essential. It could be Sunday morning with your coffee or Friday evening when the week is winding down. The key is making it a regular thing, like catching up with an old friend - except that friend is you.

Let me share some simple ways to track your progress:

Rate Your Day Scale Instead of just asking 'How was your day?' try rating different parts:

How connected did I feel to others today?
How many times did I catch myself before reacting to my old patterns?
How gentle was I with myself when things got tough?

Weekly Check-In Questions

What felt lighter this week?
What old habits showed up?
What new choices did I make?

The beauty of doing these regular check-ins is that you start noticing patterns. You may realise you're not flying off the handle as quickly as you used to. You may notice that you can finally accept help without feeling guilty. These might seem small, but they're huge wins worth celebrating. And here's something important: healing isn't a straight line. Some weeks, you might feel like you're sliding backward—and that's completely normal. Think of it like learning to dance—sometimes you step forward, sometimes back, but you're still dancing. What matters is that you're paying attention, noticing what's changing and challenging, and, most importantly, being kind to yourself along the way.

Let me share some practical tools that can help you track your healing journey. These aren't about scoring yourself - they're more like taking a gentle inventory of where you are right now.

The Emotions Weather Report Think of this like checking the weather, but for your inner world:

What's my emotional 'temperature' today? (Hot with anger? Cool and calm? Stormy with mixed feelings?)
What's my inner 'forecast' looking like? (Do I sense any emotional storms brewing?)
What's my emotional 'climate' been like lately? (Not just today, but the overall pattern)

The Body Check-In Map Our bodies often know we're healing before our minds catch up. Notice:

Where do you feel relaxed now that used to be tense?
Are you sleeping better or worse?
Has your appetite changed?
Are you holding less tension in your shoulders/jaw/stomach?
Are those old stress headaches less frequent?

The Relationships Mirror Look at how your connections with others are shifting:

Am I setting boundaries more easily?
Do I speak up more about my needs?
Can I stay calmer during disagreements?
Am I choosing to spend time with people who make me feel good about myself?
Do I recognise toxic situations more quickly now?

The Weekly Wins Journal: Each week, note down:

One old pattern you caught yourself in (awareness is the first step!)
One moment when you responded differently than you would have in the past
One kind thing you did for yourself
One boundary you maintained
One truth you told (even if it was just to yourself)

The Monthly Film Reel: At the end of each month, look back like you're watching a film of your life:

What scenes would have triggered you three months ago but feel manageable now?
What new habits are becoming part of your story?
What old scripts are you finally ready to rewrite?

Remember: You're not looking for perfection here. Some days, you might only have the energy to do a quick temperature check, and that's okay. On other days, you should dive deeper. Trust your instincts about what kind of check-in you need. The real power of these tools isn't just in using them—it's in what they tell you about your journey. They're like little love notes to your future self, showing you that you are moving forward, even when it doesn't feel like it.

Getting Your Feelings Out: When Words Aren't Enough

Do you know those feelings that are too big, messy, or complicated to describe? Sometimes, picking up a crayon or paint brush can say more than a thousand therapy sessions. I can almost hear you saying, 'I am not an artist' or 'I can't draw' - You really don't have to be. In fact, all you need to do is stop your mind from speaking to you. Most likely, your mind will be saying, 'You can't do this.' - IGNORE THAT VOICE - you can do this, and what's more, if you can just let yourself go, I promise you will enjoy this.

This is a therapy that I use a lot myself. I have found the biggest thing that helps me to let go is when I tell myself, 'I am not going to show this to **anybody; nobody** is going to have a point of view of this painting;' I don't want to know if they think it is good or bad, that is not important, this is for me, and I will enjoy the process. I don't care what the outcome is (what it looks like) as long as I enjoy it!

Just remember this isn't about creating gallery-worthy masterpieces. It's about letting your feelings flow onto paper in whatever feels right. Think of it as giving your emotions colors and shapes. Maybe your anger is spiky red lines, or your sadness is swirling blue circles. There's no 'wrong' way to do this.

The first time I tried this—I grabbed some paint and started slapping it around the paper. It looked like a toddler's artwork, but you know what? It felt good, It was really good, like finally letting out a breath I'd held for years.

Here are some simple ways to start:

Feeling Scribbles: Grab some coloured pencils or crayons and some paper. Close your eyes, think about how you're feeling, and let your hand move across the paper. Don't think too hard about it. Want to use every colour in the box? Go for it. Feel like using just black? That's fine, too.

Memory Maps: Get a piece of paper and draw or collage your childhood memories. Your happy memories are yellow sunny spots, and the harder ones are darker shadows. You might surprise yourself with what comes up.

Play with Clay There's something incredibly satisfying about squishing Clay or Play-Doh when you're processing big feelings. Roll, squash, shape, and let your hands do the talking. Sometimes, just the feeling of creating something with your hands can help ground you when emotions feel overwhelming.

Vision Boarding: Grab some old magazines, scissors, and glue. Cut out images that speak to you - don't overthink it. You may be drawn to peaceful nature scenes or strong, powerful images. Whatever catches your eye. Arrange them in a way that feels right to you. This isn't about making it pretty - it's about creating a picture of what matters to you right now.

Colour Conversations Next time you're painting, try this: Instead of thinking about what to paint, ask yourself:
What colour matches how I feel right now?
If my inner child could pick any colour, what would they choose?
What colour feels safe? What colour feels scary? Let these colours meet on the canvas and see what happens when interacting.

Emotional Weather Painting This is perfect for abstract work:
If your anxiety was a storm, what would it look like?
If your peace was a gentle rain, how would it flow?
If your strength was a sunrise, what colors would it use?

Layer Stories This one's powerful for processing past experiences:
Start with a base layer representing an old memory or feeling.
Add new layers as your feelings about it change.
Keep building layers until you feel complete. Sometimes, watching each layer partially covering up the last one is incredibly healing.

The Release Ritual This is especially good for processing difficult emotions:

Choose colours that represent what you need to let go of. Paint them however feels right - aggressive strokes, gentle washes, whatever comes, then select colours that represent healing or hope. Let these new colours transform or interact with the first ones – keep working until you feel a sense of resolution

Freedom Fingers (this is one of my favourite ways of painting) Sometimes brushes can feel too controlling. Try:

Finger painting (yes, as adults!)
Using your hands to smear and blend
Creating texture with your palms, this direct contact with the paint can be incredibly grounding and freeing.

When you're done, take a moment to look at what you've created. What colours did you use most? What shapes keep showing up? Where did you press harder with your tools, and where were you gentler? These aren't just random choices - they're little windows into your feelings.

Remember: Your art doesn't need to make sense to anyone else. It doesn't even need to make sense to you right away. Sometimes, just creating something - anything - can help you release the feelings that have been stuck inside you for too long.

Getting Free from the Weight of Guilt and Shame

Do you know that heavy feeling in your chest when you think about specific memories? That voice that whispers, 'You should have done better' or 'You're not good enough'? Those are guilt and shame talking. They're like unwanted houseguests who've stayed way too long, making themselves at home in your mind, commenting on everything you do.

We need to talk about these feelings because they have a sneaky way of running the show from behind the scenes. Maybe you find yourself saying sorry for everything (even when it's not your fault) or holding back from opportunities because that voice inside says you don't deserve good things. Maybe you've been carrying around guilt about things that happened years ago - things that everyone else has probably forgotten about but still keep you awake at night. Let me share some ways writing can help unpack these heavy emotions:

The Unsent Letter This is one of my favorites because it's so freeing. Write a letter to:

Your younger self, telling them it wasn't their fault.
Someone who hurt you (you'll never send it)
The guilt itself, telling it you're ready to let it go. Pour everything onto the page - all the messy, uncomfortable feelings. No filtering, no editing. Just let it flow.

The Forgiveness Flow Get your journal and write at the top: "I forgive myself for...' Then, keep writing. Start with small things:

For not being perfect
For the mistakes I made when I didn't know better
At times, I wasn't as strong as I thought I should be. Let each line be a small act of kindness toward yourself.

Talking Back to Your Inner Critic When that harsh voice starts, write down exactly what it says. Then write back to it, but respond as if you're talking to a friend who's being too hard on themselves. You might be surprised at how much wisdom and compassion you actually have.

The Truth Journal Sometimes shame grows because we keep things hidden. Try writing:

One truth about yourself you're afraid to share
One thing you wish others understood about you
One thing you're proud of but never talk about

<u>Remember:</u> When you start writing about guilt and shame, it might feel worse before it feels better. That's normal—you're bringing stuff that's been buried for a while to the surface. Be gentle with yourself. Light a candle, make some tea, or wrap yourself in a cosy blanket while writing. This isn't about erasing the past or pretending mistakes didn't happen. It's about finally putting down the rocks you've carried in your backpack all these years. It's about looking at yourself with kinder eyes and saying, 'Yes, that happened, and I'm still worthy of love.'

Becoming the Author of Your Own Story

Think about your favourite books - the ones you couldn't put down, you know the ones, just one more page, late into the night.) Now imagine that your life is a story, and you're not just the main character - you're also the author. Pretty powerful. Many of us have been reading from a script we didn't write - one filled with other people's expectations, old hurts, and beliefs that no longer serve us.

Your story so far has been 'I'm not good enough' or 'Bad things always happen to me.' These aren't just thoughts—they're stories we've told ourselves so many times that they feel like truth. But here's the exciting part: as the author of your life, you have the power, you have the pen. Just start and write a different version. This isn't about pretending the hard stuff never happened. It's about looking at your life's chapters through new eyes. At that time, did you feel like you had failed? That chapter's about courage - about how you dared to try something scary. The period when everything felt like it was falling apart? That may be the chapter where you discovered how strong you are.

When you share your story with people who understand, that can be incredibly healing. Whether it's in a support group, with a trusted friend, or even in an online community, there's something powerful about saying, 'This is who I am; this is what I've been through' and having someone respond with 'Me too' or 'I hear you.'

<u>Remember:</u> Your story isn't finished. Every day is a new page; you can decide what to write.

· ♥ · ♥ · ♥ · ♥ · ♥ ·

Chapter 3 Key Takeaways: Your Journey to Self-Expression

What We've Learned:

There are many ways to express and process our emotions - through art, writing, and storytelling
Creative expression can reach parts of us that words alone can't touch
Our inner critic's voice isn't the truth - it's just one version of our story
Healing can happen through many channels, and it's okay to explore until you find what works for you

Practical Tools to Try: Creative Expression

Try abstract painting when words feel too hard
Use colours to express emotions you can't name
Let your inner child play with art materials

Remember: It's about the process, not the result

Writing for Release

Write unsent letters to release old hurts
Journal about guilt and shame without judgment
Create dialogues with your inner critic
Use prompts to explore deeper feelings

Telling Your Story

Start noticing the stories you tell yourself
Practice reframing negative narratives
Share your story with trusted others

Celebrate your strength and resilience.

There's no 'right' way to express yourself
Progress isn't always linear
Every small step toward self-expression counts
You have the power to rewrite your story

Looking Ahead: In the next chapter, we'll explore deeper ways to nurture and protect your inner child as they begin to trust and open up more fully.

Chapter 4: Learning to Be Gentle with Yourself

I can clearly remember the first time I tried meditation as if it were yesterday. There I was, sitting cross-legged on my living room floor, feeling slightly ridiculous and thinking, 'This is never going to work.' My mind was racing with thoughts about work deadlines, that awkward conversation I didn't want to have, and whether I'd remembered to get something out of the freezer for dinner. But then something unexpected happened. As I followed the gentle voice of the meditation guide, everything started to slow down. It was like finally stepping out of a noisy crowd into a quiet room.

That's when I met her - that younger version of me who'd been waiting so patiently to be heard. Not in a weird, supernatural way, but I could feel her presence in those quiet moments. That part of me that still remembered what it felt like to be small and scared, still carrying around old hurts I thought I'd forgotten.

If you're now rolling your eyes and thinking, 'Meditation isn't for me,' - I get it. I was that person, too. But this isn't about sitting in perfect silence or achieving some mystical state of enlightenment. Think of it more like setting up a gentle meeting with yourself, creating a quiet space where your inner child feels safe enough to come out of hiding.

Guided meditation is just what it sounds like - someone's voice helping you navigate this inner journey. It's like having a kind friend holding your hand as you explore those rooms in your mind you've kept locked for so long. The beauty of guided meditation is that you don't have to figure it all out alone.

You need to show up and be willing to listen. The magic happens when you create a safe space in your mind—maybe a sunny garden, a warm room filled with soft pillows, or even that secret hideout you dreamed of having as a kid. Somewhere, your younger self would feel completely safe and accepted.

The Safe Place Practice – Start with something simple and comforting:

Find a quiet spot where you won't be interrupted, get comfortable (no need for a perfect lotus position - a comfy chair works fine).
Close your eyes and take three slow breaths.

Imagine opening a door to a place that feels completely safe, make it yours - add details that would have delighted you as a child –
What does it smell like?
What can you hear?
Spend a few minutes just being in this space.

The Photo Album Journey This one's especially powerful:

Get settled comfortably and close your eyes. Imagine holding a special photo album, as you open it, each page shows a moment from your childhood. Find a picture where your younger self needs comfort and imagine stepping into that photo.
What would you say to that child?
What do they need to hear?
What kind of comfort would they understand?

The Comfort Bubble is Perfect for when you're feeling overwhelmed:

Create an imaginary bubble around yourself and fill it with your favorite colour. Make it as big or small as you need. Inside this bubble, you're completely safe. Invite your inner child to join you there – just sit together; no need for words just notice how it feels to share this safe space.

Remember: Start with just 5 minutes, if your mind wanders, that's completely normal. You might feel emotional - that's okay too. Some days will be easier than others and most importantly, you can't do this wrong!

Quick Grounding When Things Feel Too Much:

Feel your feet on the floor

Notice five things you can see

Find four things you can touch

Listen for three different sounds

Notice two things you can smell

Focus on one thing you can taste

Learning to Be on Your Own Side

You know that voice in your head that's always ready with criticism? The one that jumps in with 'You should have done better' or 'What's wrong with you?' Well, this approach called ACT (Acceptance and Commitment Therapy) has helped me—and many others—lower the volume on that harsh inner critic.

Think of it as learning to be your best friend instead of your worst enemy. Most of us are experts at beating ourselves up, right? We say things to ourselves that we'd never dream of saying to someone we care about. ACT helps us change that pattern. Here's what made sense to me: Instead of pushing away those uncomfortable feelings (which never really works anyway), you learn to say, 'Okay, this feeling is here right now, and that's alright.' It's like making room for all parts of yourself - even the messy bits.

Let me share some simple ways to start:

The Thought Cloud Exercise: When you catch yourself in a spiral of negative thoughts:

Imagine each thought as a cloud in the sky, watch it float by without trying to grab it or push it away. Notice how thoughts come and go, just like clouds.

Remember: You are the sky, not the weather

The Best Friend Switch: Next time you make a mistake, before that voice in your head starts:

*Stop and ask: 'What would I say to my best friend?' Would you tell them they're stupid, or would you be understanding?
Try giving yourself that same kindness.*

This isn't about becoming perfect or never having negative thoughts again. It's about learning to treat yourself with the kindness you'd show a friend going through a tough time. Each time you catch yourself being harsh and choose gentleness instead, you're building a better relationship with yourself.

The Pause Button: When things feel overwhelming:

Take a breath and notice where you are right now – feel your feet on the ground.
Remind yourself: 'This is just a moment, and moments pass.'

Remember: You wouldn't expect a flower to grow in soil you keep poisoning with criticism. The same goes for your growth - it needs the nurturing soil of self-compassion to bloom.'

Here are some real-life ways to practice being kinder to yourself:

The Morning Mirror Moment: Next time you're getting ready and that critical voice pipes up about how you look:

Pause and catch yourself – take a breath and try saying something you'd say to a friend. Instead of 'Ugh, I look terrible. ' Try, 'Hey, you look great today.' It might feel weird at first, but that's okay. You're learning a new language of self-kindness.

The Mistake Response When you mess something up (we all do):

Notice your first reaction *('I'm so stupid' or 'I can't do anything right')* then take a moment to soften your voice -Try: *'Okay, that didn't go as planned. What can I learn from this?'*

Remember: Making mistakes doesn't make you a mistake

The Permission Slip: When you're being hard on yourself about taking care of your needs:

Write yourself an actual permission slip
'I give myself permission to rest when I'm tired.'
'I give myself permission to say no.'
'I give myself permission to ask for help.' Keep it in your wallet or take a photo of it on your phone

The Growth Album: Start collecting evidence of your progress:

Save screenshots of lovely messages people send you. Write down **all**

the small wins.
Take photos of moments you're proud of. Look through this collection on tough days to remind yourself how far you've come.

Remember: Being kind to yourself isn't selfish - it's necessary. Just like you must put your oxygen mask on first in an airplane, you must treat yourself with compassion before you can truly be there for others.

Let me share some more gentle ways to connect with your younger self:

The Time Travel Room

Imagine a special room with a big, comfy chair, in this room, there's a screen or window that can show any moment from your past. Let your younger self choose what to show you. Maybe they want to share a happy memory you've forgotten, or perhaps they need you to witness a moment when they felt alone. Just be there, watching with understanding eyes – If it feels right, imagine stepping through to give comfort or join in their joy.

The Safe House Visit: This one's perfect for tough days:

Create a cosy house with everything your inner child needs, what would make them feel completely safe and loved? Maybe there's a kitchen that always smells like cakes or a room full of soft pillows to cry in if needed. Maybe there is a playroom with all the toys they never had. Let them show you around their perfect space – notice what they've chosen to include.

The Birthday Party Redo

Imagine throwing a party for your younger self, everything is the same as they would want it. Who's invited? what games do they want to play? What kind of cake makes their eyes light up? Give them all the celebrations they might have missed. Watch them feel unique and cherished.

Remember:

Take breaks if emotions get intense

Some memories might make you cry - that's healing

Your younger self might surprise you with what they share

Trust the process - healing happens in its own time

Keep tissues nearby - sometimes tears are part of the journey

Changing Your Inner Voice: From Critic to Cheerleader

Remember that feeling when someone really believes in you? How their confidence in you makes you stand taller and feel stronger? Well, that's what we'll learn to do for ourselves. It's called using affirmations, though I like to think of them as training your inner voice to be your biggest supporter instead of your harshest critic (and I don't know about you, but mine has given me a real bashing over the years).

Do you know how a song gets stuck in your head after hearing it over and over? Our negative thoughts work the same way - they become like broken records playing in our minds. 'I'm not good enough,' 'I always mess things up,' 'I don't deserve good things.' 'I am stupid'. But here's the amazing thing: we can choose to play a different song. We can rewire our brains to play more supportive, loving messages instead.

Let's make this real. Instead of that vague 'think positive' advice, let's talk about how to actually do this:

Morning Messages: Start small. When you're brushing your teeth or making coffee, try saying:

'I've got through hard times before, and I can do it again.'
'I'm learning and growing every day.'
'It's okay to take up space in this world.'

Make them feel true for you. If saying 'I am confident' feels like a lie, try 'I'm learning to trust myself more each day' instead.

Turning Down the Inner Critic When that harsh voice pipes up:

Notice it: *'Ah, there's my old pattern talking.'*
The question is: *'Would I say this to someone I love?'*
Replace it: *'I'm doing the best I can with what I know right now.'*

Make It Stick

Put sticky notes in places only you see - your diary, inside your wardrobe. Set gentle reminders on your phone with supportive messages and write them in your journal each morning. Say them out loud when you're alone (yes, it feels weird at first - do it anyway!)

Remember: This isn't about pretending everything's perfect. It's about being as kind to yourself as you would be to a friend. Start with just one affirmation that feels true-ish. Maybe *'I deserve to take care of myself'* or *'My feelings matter.'* Say it until you start to believe it, then add another. These aren't magic spells - they're more like planting seeds. Some will take root quickly, while others might need more time and care. That's okay. You're not trying to fool yourself; you're reminding yourself of truths you might have forgotten.'

Here are some affirmations that really speak to healing your inner child. I've grouped them by different needs - pick the ones that resonate most with you:

When You're Feeling Scared or Anxious:

'I am safe now, and I can protect myself.'
'My feelings are valid, even if they're messy.'
'I don't have to be perfect to be worthy.'
'I can take small steps - I don't have to have it all figured out.'

When That Old Pain Comes Up:

'I'm allowed to feel angry about what happened.'
'It wasn't my fault - I was just a child.'
'I can hold space for both my pain and my healing.'
'I'm breaking old patterns and creating new ones.'

For Building Self-Trust:

'I trust my gut feelings.'
'I know what's best for me.'
'It's okay to change my mind.'
'I can say no without feeling guilty.'

When You Need Gentle Comfort:

'I give myself permission to rest.'
I don't have to earn love or care.'
'My needs matter.'
'I deserve gentleness and patience.'

For Growing Stronger:

'I learn from my experiences, but they don't define me.'

'I'm stronger than I think.'
'Each day, I trust myself a little more.'
'I'm writing a new story for myself.'

Tips for Using These:

Pick just one or two to start with and say them when you're doing everyday things - washing dishes, walking, or driving (you get the idea). If they bring up emotions, that's okay - let yourself feel them. Change the words to make them feel authentic to you.

Write your favourite one where you'll see it every day

Remember: Some days, these will feel true; others might feel impossible to believe. That's normal. Say them anyway. You're not trying to convince yourself - you're creating new pathways in your brain, like wearing a new path through tall grass. Each time you walk it, it gets clearer.

Finding Healing in Music: Your Soundtrack to Inner Peace

Ever notice how certain songs can take you back to a specific moment? Maybe it's hearing that song that always played in your mum's car or the one that got you through your first heartbreak. Music has this fantastic way of reaching places inside us that words can't touch. Think about how a sad song can make you feel less alone when you're hurting or how the right beat can lift your mood when you're down. Music somehow knows exactly what you're feeling, even when you can't quite explain it yourself.

Here's how you can use music to help with healing:

Create Your Healing Playlists:

The Safe Space Mix

Choose songs that make you feel completely secure. Tunes that remind you of times you felt protected. Find melodies that feel like a warm hug.

The Release Playlist

Discover songs that let you feel your anger safely. The music you can cry to when you need to, you know, those tracks that help let those big feelings out.

The Inner Child Collection

Remember the songs from your childhood that bring happy memories. Music that makes you want to dance like no one's watching, tunes that spark that playful part of you.

The Comfort Songs

This is music for when you need gentleness, melodies that help you feel understood, songs that remind you you're not alone.

How to Use Music for Healing:

Listen with headphones when you need your own space.
Play gentle music during your journal writing.
Put on upbeat songs when old sadness creeps in.
Use calming music to help you sleep.

Remember: There's no 'wrong' music for healing. That pop song that everyone makes fun of? If it speaks to your heart, it's perfect. That old lullaby that makes you tear up? It might be just what your inner child needs to hear. Trust what moves you. Sometimes healing sounds like classical music, sometimes it's heavy metal, and sometimes it's that embarrassing boy band from your teenage years. It's all valid.

Here are some more ways to let music help you heal:

The Morning Music Ritual:

Instead of checking your phone first thing, try playing one song that sets the tone for your day – having a mini dance party while getting dressed! Or try humming your favourite tune while making breakfast. It's amazing how different your day feels when it starts with music instead of scrolling.

The Emotion Release Session

When feelings get too big, find a private space where you can be loud and put on headphones (it feels safer somehow). Then play that one song that really gets you – let yourself feel everything - cry, scream into a pillow, dance it out. Follow it with a gentle, soothing song to help you calm down.

The Time Travel Playlist

This one's special for inner child work – make a playlist of songs from different ages of your life, songs from when you were tiny (maybe lullabies or kids' songs). Find music from your school years – the teen anthems that meant everything to you, then listen to the songs in order. Let yourself remember who you were at each stage, then notice what emotions come up – send love to yourself at each age.

The Bedtime Symphony

Create a special wind-down routine – Start with slightly upbeat songs to get any last energy out then gradually move to slower, calmer tunes, ending with peaceful instrumental music. Let it be like a musical blanket wrapping around you.

Remember: Some songs might bring up unexpected emotions - that's okay, If a song feels too intense, you can always skip it, your healing soundtrack will change as you do. Sometimes, the songs that heal most are the ones that make you cry. Over the years I've learned those songs that you're almost embarrassed to admit you love? They're often the ones your inner child needs most. Give yourself permission to love what you love without judgment.

Moving Your Story: When Your Body Does the Talking

You know that feeling when a song comes on, and some part of you needs to move? That's your body asking to speak. The first time I let myself dance alone in my room, I felt ridiculous - all elbows and awkward movements. But then something shifted. With my eyes closed, my body started telling stories I didn't know I was holding onto. Here's the thing about trauma and hard emotions—they don't just live in our minds. They settle into our bodies like dust in corners. Maybe you notice them in your tight shoulders, that knot in your stomach, or the way you hold your breath without realising it. Movement is like spring cleaning for these stored emotions.

TRY THIS:
DANCE LIKE NOBODY'S WATCHING (BECAUSE THEY'RE NOT) FIND A PRIVATE SPACE AND PUT ON MUSIC THAT MOVES YOU. CLOSE YOUR EYES AND LET YOUR BODY LEAD. THERE ARE NO RULES, NO RIGHT OR WRONG MOVES, JUST FOLLOW WHAT FEELS GOOD.

Morning Wake-Up:
Instead of jumping straight into your day, stretch like a cat, shake out

your hands and feet, roll your shoulders and move in whatever way your body is asking for.

The Emotion Shake-Out
When feelings get too big and are hard to handle, put on music that matches your mood. Let yourself stomp if you're angry, flow and sway if you're sad, jump and spin if you're anxious. Let your body tell its story.

Remember: This isn't about looking good or knowing how to dance. It's about letting your body help you heal.

Chapter 4 Key Takeaways: Tools for Deep Healing

What We've Learned:

Your body, mind, and emotions are all connected in your healing journey.
There are many paths to healing: meditation, affirmations, music, and movement.
Each person's healing journey looks different.
Small, consistent practices can lead to significant changes.

Practical Tools to Try:

Meditation and Visualisation.
Create your safe inner space.
Meet with your inner child regularly.
Use guided meditations when you need support.
Start small - even 5 minutes counts.
Positive Self-Talk.
Replace harsh self-criticism with gentle words.
Write affirmations that feel true to you.
Put reminders where you'll see them.
Practice self-compassion daily.
Music and Movement.
Create healing playlists for different emotions.
Use music to connect with your inner child.
Let your body move and release stored feelings.
Dance, stretch, or move in ways that feel good.

Remember:
Healing isn't linear - some days will feel more manageable than others.
Trust what works for you.
Your body holds wisdom - listen to it.
You don't have to do this perfectly.

Looking Ahead: In the next chapter, we'll explore how to maintain these practices and continue your healing journey even through challenging times.

Chapter 5: Learning to Say No (And Mean It)

Growing up in chaos teaches strange lessons about boundaries. When you've spent your childhood walking on eggshells, trying to read moods, and dodge emotional storms, you either learn to build walls so high nobody can get in or lose sight of where you end and others begin. Boundaries are not about shutting people out or letting everyone in. They're about knowing your limits, understanding what feels right and what doesn't, recognising when something makes you uncomfortable, and having the courage to say so.

When Your Warning Bells Go Quiet

The tricky thing about boundaries is that they often get crossed so slowly, subtly, that you don't notice until you're exhausted and resentful. It may start with a friend who always has a crisis right when you're about to sleep. Or family members who make little digs about your choices - 'Oh, you're wearing that?' with that tone that makes you feel two inches tall. Or the coworker who dumps their work on you because 'you're just so good at this stuff!'

These aren't just annoying moments - they're boundary violations wearing clever disguises. And the worst part? Often, they come wrapped in packages that make you feel guilty for even feeling bothered. 'I'm just trying to help!' 'Can't you take a joke?' 'Family always comes first'!

The Price We Pay

When we keep letting our boundaries get stepped on, it's like living in a house where everyone has the key except you. You start feeling anxious in your own space, always waiting for the next interruption, the next demand, the next guilt trip. Your body might start sending you signals - headaches, that knot in your stomach, trouble sleeping - but you brush them off because 'it's not that bad' or 'other people have it worse.'

Here's what helped me start noticing when my boundaries were being crossed:

The Body Check-In

Notice when your shoulders tense up around certain people.
Pay attention to that gut feeling that something's 'off.' (it's normally right).
Watch for when you start holding your breath in conversations.

Finding the Words: Speaking Up for Yourself

Let's discuss one of the hardest parts of setting boundaries—actually saying them out loud. It's one thing to know in your heart what's okay and what isn't; it's another to tell someone else, especially when you've spent years swallowing your words. I've learned that speaking your truth doesn't have to mean starting a fight. Think of it like adjusting the temperature in a room - you're not attacking anyone by saying it's too hot or too cold; you're just stating what you need to feel comfortable.

Some Ways to Start:

The Direct Approach Instead of: 'You're always barging in, and it's driving me crazy!' Try: 'I need some warning before you come over. It helps me feel more prepared.'

The Reality Check When someone says: 'Why are you being so sensitive?' You can say: "This matters to me, and I'm asking you to respect that.'

The Clear Signal: Instead of hoping people will read your mind:

'I can't talk right now, but I'll call you back when I can focus.'
'I need some time to think about that before I decide.'
'That doesn't work for me.'

Sure, some people won't like your boundaries. They might push back or try to make you feel guilty. That's good information - it tells you exactly who might not be safe to keep close in your life.

Remember: You don't need to explain or defend your boundaries. You don't need a tragic backstory or three good reasons. 'No' is a complete sentence. 'I don't want to' is enough.

This gets easier with practice, like building muscle. Start with something small, with people who feel safer. It could be telling a friend you must reschedule instead of pushing yourself to go out when you're exhausted or letting someone know that certain topics are off-limits for now.

Here are some real-life situations and ways to handle them:

The Phone Boundary When someone expects you to always answer right away:

'I keep my phone on silent during work/after 8pm.'
'I'll check messages twice a day - if it's urgent, let me know.'
Instead of feeling guilty about 'missing' calls, you're setting clear expectations.

The Energy Vampire For those people who drain you with constant drama:

'I can listen for a few minutes, but then I need to get back to what I'm doing.'
'I care about you, but I'm not the best person to help with this - have you considered talking to a counselor?'

The Space Invader: When someone keeps pushing for more than you can give:

'I need time alone to recharge - it's not about you; it's about what I need.'
'I value our relationship and need my own space.'

The Guilt Tripper When they try to make you feel bad about your boundaries:

'That's not fair,' - they say, you respond with, *'I understand you're upset, but this is what works for me.'*

Quick Responses for Tough Moments:

'Let me think about that and get back to you.'
'That doesn't work for me.'
'I'm not comfortable with that.'
'This isn't up for discussion.'

Remember: The first few times you set a boundary, your voice might shake, your heart might race, and you might feel like you're being mean or selfish. That's normal—it's just your old programming trying to keep you 'safe' by keeping you small. Do it anyway. The more you practice, the more natural it becomes.

Getting Over the Guilt of Saying No

Let's talk about that knot in your stomach when you need to set a boundary. That voice in your head that whispers, *'You're being difficult'* or *'Who do you think you are?'* I get it. When you grow up learning that love means always being available, always saying yes, and setting boundaries, it can feel like you're doing something wrong.

Maybe you learned early on that putting yourself first was 'selfish.' Perhaps you watched the adults in your life pour themselves empty trying to keep everyone else happy. Or maybe you were the one who had to be 'good,' never causing trouble, never making waves. These lessons sink deep into our bones. Here's the truth that took me years to learn: Setting boundaries isn't about being mean or selfish. It's about being honest. Think of it like this: When your phone battery is low, you charge it. Nobody calls your phone selfish for needing to recharge. You deserve the same basic care.

<u>Try These When Guilt Creeps In</u>:

'I'm not being mean; I'm being clear.'
'Taking care of myself helps me show up better for others.'
'I deserve to feel comfortable and safe.'
'Someone else's disappointment is not my emergency.'

The amazing thing is that relationships often improve when you start setting healthy boundaries (even though it feels terrifying at first). Not all of them—some people might not like the new you who knows how to say no. But the relationships that matter tend to grow stronger because they're built on honesty instead of obligation.

<u>Starting Small:</u>

Practice saying *'let me think about it'* instead of automatic yes.
Notice when you're doing something out of guilt rather than choice.
Give yourself permission to change your mind.
Remember: you don't need a 'good enough' reason to set a boundary.

Think of boundaries like the walls of your house—they don't exist to shut people out but to protect what's precious inside. Without them, anyone could walk in at any time. Trust is tricky when you've grown up in chaos. When the people who were supposed to protect you didn't, or when you learned early on that love could turn to anger in a heartbeat, trusting others feels like walking on thin ice. You're always listening for the cracks. This is what I've learned about trust - It's not about taking giant leaps of faith, It's about tiny steps, observing to see what people do with the small pieces of yourself that you share. It's like having a drawer full of broken trust from the past and slowly learning how to build something new with better materials.

What Real Trust Looks Like:

When someone says they'll do something, they do it.
They respect your boundaries without making you feel guilty.
You can tell them hard truths without fear of explosion.
They own their mistakes instead of blaming or denying.
You feel safe being yourself around them.

Building Trust Step by Step:

Start small - share little things and see how they handle them, then watch for consistency between words and actions. Notice how they treat others, not just you. Pay attention to how they handle your 'no' and trust your gut feelings - they're usually trying to tell you something (and they are normally right). When Trust Gets Broken Sometimes, even good relationships hit rough patches. If trust breaks, healing is possible, but it needs:

Honest conversations about what happened.
Actual acknowledgment of hurt (not just 'sorry you felt that way').
Apparent changes in behavior, not just promises.
Time to rebuild - you can't rush trust back into place.

Remember: Trust isn't about being perfect. It's about being honest. When someone messes up (and we all do), how they handle it matters. Do they own it? Do they try to fix it? Or do they blame, deny, or make excuses?

Opening Your Heart: Learning to Love and Be Loved

You know that flutter in your stomach when someone really sees you? Not just the carefully edited version we show the world, but the real, messy, beautiful you? That's what true intimacy feels like. It's more than just physical closeness - creating a space where both people can be completely themselves. Think of intimacy as opening the door to a room you've kept locked for a long time. Maybe you've been hurt before, or perhaps you learned early on that it wasn't safe to let people in. That's okay. Those feelings make perfect sense, given what you've been through. But something magical happens when you find someone who makes you feel safe enough to turn the key.

What Real Intimacy Looks Like:

Being able to share your thoughts without filtering them first.
Feeling safe enough to cry (or laugh until you snort) with someone.
Knowing they'll still be there even when you're not at your best.
Experiencing touch that feels nurturing rather than demanding.
Building trust takes time, and that's precisely how it should be.

Start small - share something that made you feel vulnerable today, or tell them about a dream you've never told anyone else. Watch how they respond. Do they listen? Do they hold your story gently? These little moments are the building blocks of a deeper connection. Past hurts can make this scary. You may be carrying wounds from childhood, or perhaps previous relationships left you wondering if it's worth the risk. Those fears are real, and they deserve to be acknowledged. But, you can move at your own pace. There's no rush and no timeline for opening up. The right person will understand this and respect your journey.

Try This Together:

Sit quietly together for five minutes, just being present (it's okay if it feels awkward at first!). Then write down three things you appreciate about each other and share them. Practice active listening: when one person talks about their day, the other listens - no fixing, no advice, just presence. Sometimes, it might feel like you're taking two steps forward and one step back. That's normal. Healing and opening up aren't a straight line. Each small step you take toward letting someone in is brave, even if it doesn't feel that way. You're not just learning to trust others—you're learning to trust yourself and your own heart again.

Remember, real love doesn't demand that you become someone else. It creates a space where you can be who you are, your authentic self, your quirks are celebrated, and your fears are held with gentleness. You deserve that kind of love that feels like coming home to yourself.

Breaking Old Family Patterns: A New Way Forward

Ever notice how you automatically react to your family in ways that feel like watching an old movie? Maybe you become a different version of yourself the moment you walk through your parents' door or find yourself using the exact phrases you swore you'd never say. That's because family patterns run deep - like invisible scripts we've all memorized without realising it. Think about it: if you grew up in a house where everyone bottled up their feelings, chances are you learned to do the same. Or arguments in your family always ended in slammed doors and silent treatments, and now that's your go-to move when things get tough. These patterns aren't your fault - they're more like habits you inherited along with your Mum's recipe book or Dad's old records.

Here's What We Often Carry From Family:

Ways of handling conflict (or avoiding it altogether).
Beliefs about what love should look and feel like.
Unspoken rules about which feelings are 'okay' to show.
Ideas about what makes someone 'good enough.'

But here's the good news: just because these patterns are familiar doesn't mean they're permanent. Making changes in family dynamics is like learning to dance to a different beat - it might feel awkward at first, but with practice, it starts feeling natural.

Let's Begin the Change Together:

Start by setting small boundaries for yourself, like saying, *'I need to take a break when voices get raised.'* This is a gentle way to protect your wellbeing. Practice sharing your true feelings. Instead of saying, 'You always...' try expressing, 'I felt hurt when...' This can open up space for understanding and connection. Be mindful of when you slip back into old patterns, and allow yourself to pause and reflect. It's okay to take a moment for yourself.

Remember: That feeling uncomfortable doesn't mean you're making a mistake. It's a natural part of growth.

One of the most challenging aspects of this journey is recognising that your changes might unsettle some family members. When you start to shift your behaviour, it can be tough for others, not because they don't care about you, but because change often brings uncertainty. It's like reorganising a familiar room and asking everyone to find their way in the new arrangement. This journey isn't about distancing yourself from your family or proving anyone wrong. It's about fostering new ways of being together that are healthier and more fulfilling for everyone. Sometimes, the bravest thing you can do is initiate the conversation by saying, 'Maybe there's a different way we could handle this.'

Remember, Change often begins with one person—someone willing to ask questions and take bold steps toward a new way of engaging. That person might be you. While this journey can feel exciting and daunting, know that each time you choose a different response, you are transforming your own experience and showing your family that change is possible and, ultimately, hopeful.

Awareness is Your Superpower: Navigating Family Dynamics

Breaking old patterns isn't about perfection—it's about tiny, brave moments of choice. Here's a gentle roadmap for transforming family interactions:

Give Yourself Permission to Pause:

When things feel overwhelming, it's okay to take a breath. Have a simple phrase ready like, *'I need a moment to think about this.'* This isn't weakness—it's emotional intelligence. You're giving yourself space to respond thoughtfully instead of reacting automatically.

Celebrate Every Single Step:

Notice an old family dynamic? Caught yourself before falling into a typical argument? That's huge! These tiny moments are your real victories. You rewire years of ingrained patterns each time you pause, reflect, or choose a different response.

This Journey Isn't About Blame:

Healing your family dynamics isn't about pointing fingers or proving anyone wrong. It's about creating healthier connections. Sometimes, the most powerful words are, *'I wonder if we could try approaching this differently.'*

What This Looks Like in Real Life:

It's good to start small. Try speaking up about a minor preference and pay attention to how new responses feel in your body. Be ready with a go-to phrase for moments when you feel you need space. Importantly, you should acknowledge every single moment of growth, no matter how tiny.

The Beautiful Truth:

Family change often begins with one person brave enough to do things differently. Let that person be you. It's scary and exciting—but every time you choose a new response, you're not just changing your experience but showing your entire family that healing, growth, and connection are possible.

Remember: You're not alone in this journey. Every small step matters, and you dare to create the relationships you've always wanted.

Chapter 5 Key Takeaways: Setting Boundaries and Managing Relationships

What We've Learned:

Boundaries aren't walls - they're guidelines for healthy relationships.
Your body's warning signals are trying to protect you.
Setting boundaries isn't selfish - it's necessary for wellbeing.
Some relationships will change when you start setting boundaries.
Guilt is usual but shouldn't drive your decisions.

Practical Things To Try

Body Check-In Practice
Notice physical tension or unease.
Pay attention when your 'warning bells' go quiet.
Trust your gut feelings.
Take time to pause before responding.

Boundary Setting Basics

Start with small, manageable boundaries.
Practice saying, 'Let me think about it' instead of immediate yes.
Use clear, direct language.

Remember: You don't need to justify your boundaries.

Managing Different Boundary Challenges

Energy Vampires: limit time and protect your energy.
Space Invaders: establish precise personal space needs.
Guilt Trippers: recognize manipulation tactics.
Phone Boundaries: set specific times for availability.

Dealing with Guilt

Notice when you're acting from guilt versus choice.
Use positive self-talk when guilt creeps in.

Remember: Someone else's disappointment isn't your emergency.

Give yourself permission to change your mind!

Remember:
Your needs matter just as much as others.
Healthy boundaries create stronger relationships.
It's okay if some people don't like your boundaries.
Progress isn't perfect - keep practicing.

Looking Ahead: In the next chapter, we'll explore how to maintain these healthy boundaries while nurturing the relationships that matter most to you.

Make a Difference with Your Review

Unlock the Power of Sharing

"HEALING YOURSELF IS CONNECTED WITH HEALING OTHERS." - YOKO ONO

Have you ever read something that just clicked? Like a lightbulb switching on in your mind, helping you see yourself in a new way? That's the magic of understanding your inner child. And that's why your review matters.

Right now, someone out there is looking for answers, wondering why they keep feeling stuck in the same old patterns. They might be holding onto hurt they don't even realise is there. But they don't know where to start.

THAT'S WHERE YOU COME IN.

Most people choose books based on reviews. A few simple words from you could be the sign they need to begin their healing journey.

Leaving a review costs nothing, takes less than a minute, and could change someone's life. Your review might help…

- One more person finally understand their emotions.
- One more parent breaks a cycle and creates a loving home.
- One more friend offers better support to someone they love.
- One more soul feels a little less alone.

> To share your thoughts and make a difference, simply scan the QR code on the following page and leave a review.

Your voice matters. Your experience matters. Together, we can help more people find their way back to themselves.

Thank you for being part of this journey.

Just CLICK HERE to leave your review or you can review using the QR code

If you love helping others, you're my kind of person. Thank you from the bottom of my heart!

Summer Weston

Chapter 6: Healing Through Your Body

Have you ever noticed how your shoulders creep up toward your ears during stressful times? Or how your stomach tightens when you're worried? That's not just in your head—it's your body telling a story. I learned this firsthand when I discovered somatic healing. Up until then, I thought healing was all about talking through my problems, but my body had other ideas.

Think of trauma like an ice cube tray that's been left in the freezer for too long. Even after you empty it, the shape of what was there remains. That's how our bodies hold onto difficult experiences - in tight muscles, shallow breathing, or that knot in your stomach that never entirely disappears. Amazingly, your body remembers everything, even the stuff your mind has filed away in dusty folders marked 'deal with later.'

Why Our Bodies Keep Score:

When something scary or overwhelming happens, our bodies react and think later. These reactions (like tensing up or holding our breath) can get stuck on 'replay.' Over time, we might stop noticing these patterns - they become our new normal, but our bodies keep trying to tell us something's not quite right. The science behind this is pretty incredible. Researchers have found that our bodies don't just respond to our thoughts—they actually store memories in our muscles and tissues. Each cell becomes a tiny storage unit for experiences we haven't fully processed yet. That's where somatic healing comes in—it's like having a conversation with your body instead of just about your body.

Ways Your Body Might Be Speaking: Somatic Healing

You may feel chronic tension in certain areas (that massage can't quite fix) or constantly feeling like you need to be 'on guard.' Maybe digestive issues that come and go? You could be feeling disconnected from your body, like you're just a head floating around. The good news? Your body wants to heal. Just like a cut knows how to scab over and repair itself, your body knows how to release old hurts - it just needs the right conditions and support. Think of somatic healing as learning a new language - the language your body has been speaking all along.

Simple Ways to Start Listening:

Notice how different emotions feel in your body (Where do you feel joy? Anger? Fear?).
Please pay attention to what makes your body feel safe and what makes it tense up.
Start with just 30 seconds of paying attention to your breathing.
Give yourself permission to move in ways that feel good, even if they look silly.

Somatic healing is so powerful because it doesn't require you to talk about everything that's ever hurt you. Sometimes, words aren't enough anyway. Instead, it's about creating a safe space for your body to tell its story at its own pace. As you practice this kind of healing, you might find that the physical tension you've carried for years starts to melt away. You might sleep better, feel more energetic, or feel more at home in your own skin.

Remember: This isn't about forcing anything. Your body has been protecting you all this time, doing its best with what it knew. You're learning to work with it instead of pushing through or ignoring its signals. Think of it as becoming friends with your body again - maybe for the first time.

A Gentle Journey Through Your Body (A Guided Somatic Practice)

Find a quiet moment where you won't be interrupted. You should have a journal nearby to write down what you discover.

Getting Started:
Take a comfortable seat or lie down. There is no need to force a perfect position—make sure you feel supported. When you're ready, let your eyes close softly.

Let's Begin:
Take three slow breaths, just letting your body settle. There's no rush, no

pressure to feel anything specific.

Now, with gentle curiosity, let's explore:

Your Head and Face

Notice your forehead - is it relaxed or holding tension?
Feel your jaw - many of us carry stress here.
Are your facial muscles tight or soft?
Just notice, without trying to change anything.

Moving Down

Bring awareness to your neck and shoulders.
Are they lifted or relaxed?
Is one side different from the other?
What sensations do you notice?

Your Upper Body

Feel your chest - how is your breathing?
Notice your back - where does it touch the surface beneath you?
Are there places that feel tight? Places that feel at ease?
Just acknowledge whatever you find.

Your Middle

Bring attention to your stomach area.
Notice if it feels relaxed, tense, or something else.
Is there movement here as you breathe?
What emotions might be stored in this space?

Lower Body

Feel your hips and pelvis.
Notice your legs - any tension or heaviness?
Are your feet connected to the ground?
Just observe the sensations.

Before Opening Your Eyes:

Take a moment to notice which areas called out for attention.
Where did you feel most comfortable?
Where did you feel disconnected or discomfort?
What emotions came up during this exploration?

Closing the Practice:

Take a deep breath and slowly open your eyes when you're ready. Consider writing down:
Three areas where you noticed tension?
Any emotions that surfaced?
Parts of your body that felt peaceful?
Questions or insights that came up?

Remember: There's no 'right' way to feel, as every sensation has a story to tell. Your body speaks in its own language, and somatic healing is just the beginning of the conversation. This practice isn't about fixing or changing anything but listening and learning. You can return to it anytime; each experience might be different, which is perfectly normal.

Consider this your first step in understanding your body's language. Learning any new language takes time and patience, but every attempt at listening helps build that connection.

The Magic of Breathing: Your Built-in Calm Button

Ever notice how a deep sigh can feel like pressing a reset button? That's not an accident. Your breath might be the most powerful tool you have for healing - and it's been right under your nose this whole time (pun intended!). When I first learned about breathwork, I really didn't realise how powerful it could be. How could something as simple as breathing differently make a real difference? But here's the fantastic thing: your breath is like a remote control for your nervous system. Have you noticed that your breathing gets shallow and quick when you're stressed? When you're calm, it's slower and deeper. But here's the cool part - you can work this in reverse. By changing how you breathe, you can change how you feel.

Why Breathing Matters:

It's your body's natural stress-relief system.
You can use it anywhere, anytime (and it's totally free!)
It helps quiet those racing thoughts.
It brings you back to the present moment when anxiety pulls you into the future.

Let's Talk About Different Ways to Breathe:

These exercises are like different tools in your calm-down toolkit. Start with the one that feels most comfortable, and remember - there's no such thing as doing this wrong.

Belly Breathing - Think of your belly like a balloon - when you breathe in, it should expand. Perfect for Bedtime or when anxiety feels high, this deep breathing tells your body 'everything's okay' and helps turn off the stress response.

Place one hand on your belly.
Breathe in through your nose, making your belly expand like a balloon.
Breathe out through your mouth, letting your belly sink back down.
Keep your shoulders relaxed.
Do this for 5-10 breaths.

Think of it like giving your insides a gentle massage.

Alternate Nostril Breathing - This one might feel weird at first (and maybe don't try it in public!), but it's like hitting the balance button for your mind. It's perfect when you're feeling scattered or overwhelmed. This powerful breathing technique helps.

Balance your nervous system
Reduce stress
Improve mental clarity
Promote emotional calm
Enhance overall well-being

Hand Position

Use your right thumb to close the right nostril.
Use your right ring finger to close the left nostril.

Step-by-Step Technique

Firstly, find a comfortable sitting position and ensure your spine is straight. Relax your shoulders, close your eyes, and take a few natural breaths.
Bring your right hand to your nose and rest your index and middle fingers gently between your eyebrows. Your thumb should be near your right nostril, and the ring finger should be near your left nostril.

Exhale completely,
Close the right nostril with your thumb,
Inhale through the left nostril.
Close your left nostril with your ring finger,
Open your right nostril, exhale through your right nostril,
Inhale through your right nostril,
Close right nostril,
Exhale through left nostril.

Complete Cycle

Repeat this sequence 5-10 times.
Move slowly and gently.
Focus on smooth, even breathing.

Common Mistakes to Avoid

Don't force the breath.
Keep breathing soft and natural.
Don't strain.
Stop if you feel dizzy.

Emotional Benefits:

Reduces anxiety.
Calms racing thoughts.
Improves emotional balance.
Increases mental clarity.

Physical Benefits:

Lowers heart rate.
Reduces blood pressure.
Improves lung capacity.
Enhances respiratory function.

Precautions – Avoid if you have:

Serious respiratory conditions.
Recent nasal surgery.
Chest infections.
Severe anxiety or panic disorders.
Always consult a healthcare professional if unsure.

Practice Tips

Start with 3-5 cycles.
Gradually increase to 10 cycles.
Practice daily for best results.
Morning is an ideal time.
Be patient with yourself.

Remember: Breathing is a journey of self-discovery. There's no perfect way, only your way.

Calming Breath Patterns—Remember 4-7-8? Breathe in for 4, hold for 7, and out for 8. It's like a lullaby for your nervous system. Your body can't help but relax when you do this.

The Reset Breath - Perfect for Quick calm in stressful moments (like before a meeting or during a busy day)

Breathe in through your nose for 4 counts.
Hold gently for 4 counts.
Breathe out through your mouth for 4 counts.
Repeat 3-4 times.

Think of it as pressing the reset button on your nervous system.

Ocean Wave Breathing - Perfect for Breaking out of thought spirals

Breathe in through your nose.
As you exhale through your mouth, make a soft "haaa" sound.
Keep your mouth closed, but maintain that ocean-like sound.
Let each breath be like a wave, flowing in and out.

Think of it as being at the beach, letting each wave wash away tension.

Rescue Box Breathing - Perfect for Panic moments or when feeling overwhelmed.

Trace a square in front of you with your finger
Up: Breathe in for 4,
Across: Hold for 4,
Down: Breathe out for 4,
Across: Hold for 4,

Think of it like Building a box of calm around yourself.

Tension Release Breath - Perfect for Releasing physical tension

Take a deep breath in,
Hold it while you tense your whole body,
Exhale with a big sigh, letting everything go loose,
Let your body be heavy,
Think of it like wringing out a wet towel and then letting it fall soft.

Tips for Success:

Imagine your breath is like waves on a beach—coming in and going out. There is no need to force anything.

Here's the thing about breathing - you're already doing it. You've been doing it your whole life. Now, you're just learning to use it as the powerful tool it is. Think of it like discovering your smartphone has had this amazing feature all along, and you're just now learning how to use it.

The Real Magic:

When you're having a tough moment, your breath is always there. When anxiety is climbing, taking a few slow breaths can help you step back from the edge. When emotions feel too big, your breath can give you space to process them. It's like having a pause button for life's overwhelming moments.

Remember: You don't have to be perfect at this - Just notice:

How does the air feel coming in? Is it cool?
Where do you feel the breath in your body?
What happens if you slow down just a little?

Even a few conscious breaths make a difference; your breath is always with you, and you are ready to help. The most straightforward tools are often the most powerful. Your breath is like a faithful friend who's been waiting to help you all along. It's patient, always available, and never judges. It may be time to get reacquainted - Practice when you're calm so it's easier during stress.

Tips for Success:

Start with just 2-3 minutes

Your mind will wander - that's normal
If you feel dizzy, return to normal breathing

Making It Part of Your Day:

Morning: Try balloon breathing before getting out of bed

Work: Use box breathing between tasks

Evening: Ocean wave breathing to wind down

Stress: Reset breath whenever you need it

<u>Remember</u>: These exercises are like having different songs for different moods. Some days, you'll need the quiet calm of balloon breathing; others, you might need the more potent relief of tension-release breaths. Trust what your body asks for.

Energy Healing: Another Path to Inner Peace

Remember when, as a kid, you bumped your knee and someone offered to 'kiss it better'? Something about that caring attention actually helped, even though nothing physically changed. Energy healing works in a similar way—it's about directing caring attention to parts of ourselves that need support, but on a deeper level.

The first time I encountered Reiki, my friend Sharon introduced me to it. Initially, I thought it was really weird—after all, how could something you can't even see make a difference? But do you know what?, just like you can feel the tension in a room after an argument (how is that even possible!!) or the warmth of someone's love without being touched, I could actually *'feel'* the energy! there's more to healing than what we can see or measure.

What's Really Happening in Energy Healing:

Think of it like clearing a clogged pipe—but for your emotions. It's similar to acupuncture but without the needles. The practitioner works with your body's natural energy centers—it's like a deep reset for your nervous system. Imagine seven spinning wheels of energy running from the base of your spine to the top of your head. These are your chakras, and each one relates to different parts of your life:

Root: Your sense of safety and security
Belly: Your emotions and creativity
Solar Plexus: Your confidence and personal power
Heart: Love and compassion
Throat: Speaking your truth
Third Eye: Intuition and Wisdom
Crown: Connection to something bigger than yourself

Try This at Home: Even without formal training, you can work with your own energy:

Find a quiet moment,
Place your hands over your heart,
Breathe slowly and imagine warm, healing light,
Notice any sensations or temperature changes,
Stay here as long as it feels good.

When Energy Healing Might Help:

After emotional upheavals.
When you feel stuck.
During times of transition.
To support other healing work, you're doing.
When you need deep relaxation.

Remember: This isn't about replacing other types of care, and you don't need to understand exactly how it works. You may also find your experience might be different from someone else's and that small shifts can lead to significant changes. Think of energy healing like cleaning your windows—sometimes, you don't realise how cloudy things have become until you clear them. It's not about fixing what's broken but rather about removing the blocks that keep you from feeling your best. The best part? You don't have to believe in it for it to help. Just like you don't need to understand precisely how aspirin works to get relief from a headache, you can benefit from energy healing simply by being open to the experience.

Finding Peace in the Great Outdoors

Have you ever paused to notice how being outside can transform your mood? It's remarkable how your shoulders can feel lighter when you hear the gentle songs of the birds or how your mind can quiet down while you watch the leaves sway in the breeze. It's almost as if Nature has a special way of wrapping us in its comforting embrace. I can relate to those moments of tranquility. I remember standing still, surrounded by the cheerful chirping of birds, as I watched the sunset paint the sky in stunning hues. In that peaceful moment, I realised I hadn't looked at my phone in hours. Moments like these remind us how Nature can help us reset, inviting us back to a place of simplicity and authenticity.

Why Nature Heals:

It slows down our racing thoughts.
Gives our senses a break from screens and noise.
Reminds us we're part of something bigger.
Helps us breathe more deeply without even trying.

The Japanese have a beautiful practice called forest bathing (Shin-rin-yoku). Don't let the fancy name fool you - it's simply about being in Nature without a goal. You're not trying to hit 10,000 steps or get somewhere specific. You're just like a cat lounging in a sunbeam, soaking it all in.

Simple Ways to Get Your Nature Fix:

Morning Minutes

Step outside first thing with your coffee or tea and feel the air on your skin. Listen to the world waking up –
just 5 minutes can improve your whole day.

Lunch Break Reset

Find a patch of grass or a nearby tree, take off your shoes if you can and let your feet connect with the earth – eat mindfully in the fresh air.

Window Garden

No outdoor space? No problem, put some plants where you can see them and watch them grow and change. Let them remind you that growth takes time.

Weather Watching

Notice the clouds moving,

Feel the rain or wind,
Watch shadows shift,
Remember, you're part of this changing world.

The beautiful thing about Nature is that it doesn't care if you have a bad hair day or miss a deadline. It's just there, accepting and constant. The trees don't judge your progress.

Start small - even 10 minutes matters
Use all your senses
Notice what draws your attention
Let yourself be curious

Remember: You don't need special equipment and there's no "wrong" way to do this. Nature is everywhere, even in cities – every little bit of outdoor time counts.

Your Reflection Moment:

Think about a time when being outside made you feel better. Maybe it was watching a sunset, or feeling rain on your face, or smelling fresh-cut grass. What did you notice? How did your body feel? What changed in your mind?

Write down:

Where were you?
What caught your attention?
How did you feel different afterward?
What's one small way you could get more of that feeling this week?

Nature isn't just a nice addition to healing - it's one of our oldest and wisest teachers. It shows us that growth isn't always visible; storms pass, and every season has its purpose. It may be time to let it teach you, too.

Healing Through Scent: Your Nose Knows

Have you ever caught a whiff of something - maybe fresh cookies or pine trees - and suddenly found yourself transported to a memory? That's not just a coincidence. Your nose has a direct hotline to the emotional center of your brain, making scent one of your most potent tools for feeling better.

Your Scent Toolkit:

Here are some essential oils that can help in different ways (think of them like emotional speed dial buttons):

Lavender: The Calm Button

Perfect for: Winding down after a rough day.
How it helps: Soothes anxiety, helps with sleep.
Ways to use: On your pillow, in a bath, or in a diffuser.
Think of it as a gentle hug for your nervous system.

Peppermint: The Wake-Up Call

Perfect for: Fighting brain fog.
How it helps: Boosts focus, clears your head.
Ways to use: In your morning shower or at your desk.
Think of it as coffee for your nose.

Eucalyptus: The Deep Breath

Perfect for: When you feel stuck or stagnant.
How it helps: Opens airways, refreshes your mind.
Ways to use: In steamy showers or when you need clarity.
Think of it as Nature's version of 'clear cache.'

Simple Ways to Start:

Morning Ritual

Add a drop of energizing oil to your shower floor and let the steam carry the scent – start your day with an aromatherapy boost.

Desk Helper

Keep a small bottle of peppermint nearby and take a quick sniff when your focus dips – Use it as a natural pick-me-up.

Bedtime Magic

Put a drop of lavender on your pillowcase to create a relaxing scent bubble around you and let it guide you off to sleep.

Safety Tips (Because Your Nose Is Important):

- Always dilute oils before putting them on the skin.

- Start with less - you can always add more.

- If it smells too strong, it probably is.

- Keep oils away from pets (they're more sensitive than we are).

Remember:
Different scents work differently for everyone.
Your mood might change which scents you need.
Trust your nose - if you don't like a smell, don't use it.
Small amounts can have significant effects.

The best part about aromatherapy is that it works even without thinking about it. Unlike many healing tools that require your full attention, scent works its magic in the background, gently shifting your mood and energy while you go about your day.

Getting Started:

Pick one scent that calls to you and one simple way to use it. It could be lavender on your pillow or peppermint on your desk. Start there and notice what changes. Your nose will guide you to what works best.

Crystal Healing: Earth's Glittering Helpers

Remember collecting pretty rocks as a kid? There was something magical about finding that perfect stone - smooth, sparkly, or uniquely shaped. That childlike wonder isn't so different from how people have felt about crystals throughout history. From ancient Egyptian tombs to modern meditation rooms, these earth-made treasures have always caught our eye and captured our imagination.

Why Crystals?

Think of crystals like Nature's mood rings. Each one has its own personality and potential to help in different ways. Some feel grounding, like holding a piece of the earth, and others seem to radiate calm or energy, but each one can be a physical reminder of what you're working toward.

Popular Crystals and Their Special Vibes:

Amethyst: The Calm Keeper

What it looks like: Purple and dreamy.
Known for: Helping with sleep and peace.
Good for: Bedside tables or meditation corners.
Think of it as Your spiritual security blanket.

Rose Quartz: The Heart Helper

What it looks like: Soft pink and gentle
Known for: Opening hearts and healing hurts
Good for: Self-love and relationships
Think of it as A hug in stone form

Citrine: The Joy Jewel

What it looks like: Golden and sunny
Known for: Bringing in good vibes
Good for: Workspaces and creativity corners
Think of it as Bottled sunshine

Getting Started with Crystals:

With crystals, you can choose what calls to you and trust your instincts. Don't overthink it; pick the ones you are drawn to (you will feel it in your gut). Crystals like to be kept happy - give them a moonlight bath now and again. Occasionally, they must be cleaned gently with water (be careful to check if that is safe as some will dissolve!). Don't hide them away; keep them where you will see them. So how do you use them? You can hold one while you are meditating, put it on your desk or next to your bed, carry a small one in your pocket, or even create a pretty display that makes you smile.

<u>**Remember:**</u> There's no 'wrong' way to use crystals. You don't have to spend a lot of money on them, and it's okay to think they are pretty. Your intention matters more than rules.

The Real Magic:

Crystals work because they're natural worry stones, giving us something tangible to hold onto when life feels wobbly. They may also work because they remind us to pause and breathe, or simply because they're beautiful pieces of earth that connect us to something bigger than ourselves.

Using Crystals in Real Life:

Feeling anxious? Hold a smooth piece of amethyst
Need focus? Put a clear quartz on your desk
Want more self-love? Keep rose quartz by your mirror
Seeking peace? Create a small crystal corner in your room.

Think of crystals as tools in your emotional first-aid kit. They might not fix everything, but they can be lovely reminders of your intentions and goals. Plus, they make beautiful decorations that actually mean something.

♥ · ♥ · ♥ · ♥ · ♥

Chapter 6 Key Takeaways: Advanced Healing Tools

What We've Learned:

Healing happens on multiple levels—physical, emotional, and energetic. Our bodies store memories and emotions that need gentle release. Nature and breath are powerful, accessible healing tools, and using simple practices can create profound shifts. Remember that each person's healing journey is unique.

Practical Tools to Try:

Somatic (Body-Based) Healing

Practice regular body scans
Notice where you hold tension
Listen to your body's signals
Move in ways that feel good

Breathwork Practices

Reset Breath (4-4-4)
Balloon Belly Breathing
Box Breathing
Ocean Wave Breath
Tension Release Breath

Nature Connection

Morning minutes outside
Barefoot grounding
Mindful walks
Weather watching
Window gardens

Energy Work

Self-Reiki hand positions
Chakra Awareness
Energy check-ins
Creating quiet space

Aromatherapy

Morning energizing scents
Calming bedtime rituals
Desk focus boosters
Emotional support blends

Remember:

Start small and build slowly
Trust what works for you
Combine techniques that feel right
Be patient with the process
Every little practice counts

Looking Ahead:

In the next chapter, we'll explore how to maintain these practices in daily life and what to do when healing feels challenging.

Chapter 7: Growing Through the Hard Times & Putting Together Your Toolkit

Healing isn't about erasing your past—it's about understanding how childhood experiences shaped you and discovering the strength that carried you through. When you've grown up in chaos, survival becomes your first language, and every day is a lesson in resilience.

Understanding Your Survival Toolkit

The skills you developed weren't weaknesses—they were sophisticated survival strategies. Growing up with addiction, violence, and instability taught you remarkable abilities that most people will never understand: You were reading emotional landscapes before you could read books and learned to become invisible when safety demanded it. You learned that you were capable of protecting others at the cost of your own vulnerability. You probably developed an almost superhuman sense of anticipation and maybe even felt a lot older than you were because you were managing responsibilities far beyond your years.

These survival skills were your armour, your protection. They kept you alive when the world felt overwhelmingly dangerous. But now, it's time to recognise that the very strategies that protected you might be holding you back from the peace and connection you deserve.

Actionable Steps to Build Your Ongoing Roadmap to Healing:

1. Acknowledge your past without letting it define your future.

2. Practice self-compassion for the child who carries adult burdens.

3. Recognise that your Hypervigilance was a superpower of survival.

4. Begin to separate past threats from present realities.

5. Allow yourself to feel the full range of emotions you suppressed.

Here are detailed strategies for each of those healing steps to begin building your roadmap:

Journaling Technique: Create two columns - In the left column, write down past experiences that hurt you. In the right column, write how those experiences made you stronger. Your goal is to reframe trauma as a source of resilience, not a limitation.

Narrative Reshaping Exercise - Write your life story as if you're the hero, not the victim, and highlight the moments of survival, creativity, and strength - Focus on how you adapted and protected yourself.

Practice Self-Compassion for Your Inner Child

Mirror Work: Look at yourself in the mirror and speak to your reflection as you would to a wounded child. Use gentle phrases like 'You did the best you could.' Acknowledge the pain without judgment.

Speak to your Inner Child Meditation: Visualise yourself when you experienced the most pain and imagine holding and comforting that younger version of you. Tell them, 'You are safe now. You are loved. You are enough.'

Recognize Hypervigilance as a Survival Superpower

Reframing Exercise: List all the ways your Hypervigilance protected you, e.g., Sensing danger before it escalated, protecting siblings, and managing complex emotional landscapes. Acknowledge these as incredible survival skills.

Gradual Nervous System Regulation:

Practice grounding techniques
Learn to distinguish between actual threats and perceived threats
Deep breathing exercises

Body scan meditations
Mindfulness practices

Begin to Separate Past Threats from Present Realities

Threat Assessment Worksheet: Create a chart with columns - Perceived Threat, Actual Current Risk, Rational Response

Example**:**

Perceived Threat: 'Someone will hurt me'
Actual Current Risk: Low (in current safe environment)
Rational Response: Recognize safety, practice self-soothing

The reality-checking practice can be used when you are feeling triggered. Ask yourself, 'Is this danger real right now?' 'What evidence do I have that I am not safe', and 'what would a supportive friend say?'

Allow Yourself to Feel Suppressed Emotions

Here are some emotional release techniques:

Expressive Writing: Set a timer for 15 minutes and write without stopping or editing. Let all your emotions flow without any judgment.

Creative Expression: As discussed in other chapters, if you are in a creative mindset, you should paint, draw, dance, and make music.

Emotional Mapping: this is a personal tool that helps you understand where and how emotions live in your body, recognise emotional patterns, develop greater emotional intelligence, and create a deeper connection with your inner experiences. All you need is a large piece of paper, coloured markers or pencils, a quiet, comfortable pace, and your journal for reflection.

Draw a simple outline of a human body. You will use this for your emotional exploration. Below, I have listed different emotions and their physical locations that you can use to help you in this exercise.

Anxiety: Often feels like tightness in the chest, churning in the stomach
Sadness: Heavy feeling in the chest, the tension in the throat
Anger: Heat in the chest, clenched jaw, tight shoulders
Fear: Tingling in hands, tightness in the stomach
Joy: Lightness in chest, warmth in heart area

Grief: Hollow feeling in the chest, weight on shoulders
Red for intense emotions
Blue for calm emotions
Green for healing emotions
Swirls: Spinning or cycling emotions
Dots: Pinpointed intense feelings
Waves: Fluid, changing emotions
Sharp lines: Cutting or intense emotions

TRY THIS: CLOSE YOUR EYES AND BREATHE DEEPLY. THINK OF A RECENT EMOTIONAL EXPERIENCE AND NOTICE WHERE YOU FEEL THE EMOTION IN YOUR BODY. USE COLOURS TO REPRESENT DIFFERENT EMOTIONS AND DRAW OR COLOR THESE SENSATIONS ON YOUR BODY OUTLINE. CREATE A SCALE FROM 1 TO 10 (1 BEING BARELY NOTICEABLE, 5 MODERATE, AND 10 OVERWHELMING EMOTIONAL EXPERIENCES), THEN MARK THE INTENSITY OF EACH EMOTION ON YOUR MAP.

Create a new map each week and notice how the emotional locations change—look for patterns in your emotional landscape. This is a living document to be used as a tool of self-discovery. Remember, there is no 'right' way to create an emotional map. Your journey is valid, your feelings are important, and this process is about gentle self-exploration. I would recommend weekly for beginners and bi-weekly for experienced mappers.

After creating your map, ask yourself some reflection questions

What surprised me about my emotional experience?
Are there emotions I struggle to feel?
How do my emotions move through my body?
What triggers intense emotional responses?
When I feel anxious, I notice...
Anger feels like... in my body.

This framework provides a compassionate, structured approach to healing. Each strategy can be adapted to your personal journey, allowing flexibility and gentleness in your recovery process.
Stop if you feel overwhelmed, and seek professional support if needed.

Key takeaways from Chapter 7:

What We Have Learned

Survival Skills Are Strengths
Reframing Trauma as Resilience
The Emotional Mapping Journey
Actionable Healing Strategies
The Power of Gentle Self-Exploration
Healing is not about perfection
Acknowledging your experiences without judgment
Celebrating your survival
Creating space for your emotions
Developing self-compassion
Recognising your inherent worth

Ongoing Growth

Remember:
Your healing journey is unique
There's no "right" way to process trauma
Small steps are significant progress
Professional support is always an option
You are worthy of love, safety, and healing.

Guiding Principle: Your childhood survival skills were remarkable. You're learning to transform those skills into compassion, self-love, and genuine connection.

Looking ahead, in the next chapter, we will discuss how the inner child can affect one's professional life and how to deal with that.

• ♥ • ♥ • ♥ • ♥ • ♥ •

Chapter 8: Navigating Professional Life While Healing Your Inner Child

The Survival Dance of Work and Worth

I have worked since I was twelve years old. Money wasn't just paper and coins—it was survival. The need to earn wasn't a choice but a lifeline I've carried since childhood. At first, part-time jobs squeezed between school hours, then full-time work the moment I could legally clock in. For 25 years, I worked for the Civil Service, my entire existence seemingly controlled by the constant worry of money. As a lone parent with two children for nine years, every month's pay was a lifeline. Every additional overtime, every extra responsibility, was another thread in the safety net I was desperately trying to weave for my kids. Money wasn't just currency—it was security, protection, and hope. The fear of 'not having enough' wasn't just a financial concern. It was a deep, visceral terror that echoed the instability of my childhood.

This is how childhood trauma shows up in our professional lives—not as a distant memory, but as a constant companion, whispering strategies of survival into every work interaction, every career choice, and every professional relationship. For me, during those years of being a single parent to two little girls, survival meant working twice as hard—a full-time job and a part-time job—to ensure my children had more than I ever did. Luxuries? Those were for other people. But here's the truth no one tells you: those years of constant work wasn't just about earning money. They were about something deeper. Something more profound than paying bills. They were about proving my worth, surviving, and protecting those I loved. Every extra hour, every additional job was a shield I built against the uncertainty I'd known growing up.

Our professional lives aren't separate from our healing journey. They're another landscape where our inner child lives, breathes and sometimes struggles. The survival strategies we developed in childhood don't magically disappear when we put on our work clothes. They follow us, whispering their old stories in boardrooms, during performance reviews, and in every professional interaction.

This chapter is about understanding those whispers about recognising how childhood wounds dance through our professional lives, creating invisible barriers and unexpected strengths.

Understanding Workplace Trauma Responses: The Survival Patterns We Carry

When you've grown up learning that your worth is measured by your productivity, the workplace becomes more than just a place of employment. It's a battlefield where your deepest insecurities and most powerful survival skills play out.

People-Pleasing: The Invisible Armor

For those of us who grew up in unstable environments, people-pleasing isn't a weakness—it's a sophisticated survival strategy. In the workplace, this looks like:

Taking on extra projects without hesitation.
Difficulty saying no to additional responsibilities.
The constant fear of disappointing others.
Believing your value is directly tied to your usefulness.

Imposter Syndrome: The Echoes of Childhood Criticism

Every performance review becomes a trigger, every new challenge a potential exposure to your 'fraudulent' self. The critical voice from childhood doesn't disappear—it transforms, finding new stages to play out its narrative of inadequacy. This has been a big one for me in my life and probably the one that I have really struggled to overcome. Even now, it sometimes rears it's ugly head and I have to challenge the critical thought and find the evidence to prove that the thought is wrong.

Emotional Triggers in Professional Environments

Workplace scenarios can unexpectedly activate childhood wounds:

A stern manager reminds you of a critical parent.
Collaborative projects trigger old family dynamics.
Performance feedback resonates with childhood shame.
Competitive environments reawaken feelings of never being 'enough.'

Healing Strategies for Professional Growth

Boundary Setting: Your New Professional Superpower

Practice saying 'no' without guilt.
Recognise that your worth isn't determined by constant availability.
When you understand that setting boundaries is an act of self-respect, not rebellion.

Negotiation as Self-Care

Your salary is not just money—it's a reflection of your value
Prepare for salary discussions with the same care you'd prepare for protecting your inner child

Remember: Asking for what you deserve is not selfish

Rebuilding Professional Confidence: More Than Just Skills

Professional confidence isn't about degrees or technical expertise when you've grown up managing family chaos. It's about survival skills that most people will never understand. You learned to read emotional landscapes before you could read job descriptions. You developed an almost superhuman ability to anticipate needs, manage impossible situations, and keep everything running when the world felt like it was falling apart. These aren't just professional skills—they're survival strategies you've carried since childhood. The hypervigilance that helped you navigate a volatile home environment? That's now your secret weapon in workplace dynamics. Your ability to predict emotional storms, stay calm when others panic, and take responsibility when no one else will are extraordinary professional strengths.

But here's the complicated truth: the same survival skills that protected you can also hold you back. People-pleasing isn't professional dedication. Overworking isn't the same as adding value. Constantly proving your worth isn't the same as genuine professional growth.

Healing-informed career choices mean something profound. They mean:

Recognising your worth isn't determined by your productivity.
Understanding that your value extends beyond what you can do for others.
Learning to build professional relationships based on mutual respect, not survival.
Creating boundaries that protect your emotional energy.
Choosing work that aligns with your authentic self, not just your survival mechanisms.

This isn't about changing who you are. It's about honoring the incredible resilience that got you this far and creating space for a new way of existing professionally. Your childhood taught you how to survive. Now, it's time to learn how to thrive.

Here's a comprehensive guide to help you navigate workplace challenges:

Navigating the Professional Landscape: Practical Tools for Healing

Understanding Workplace Triggers

Before you can heal, you need to recognise your triggers. Most people who've experienced childhood trauma carry invisible emotional baggage into their professional lives.

Workplace Trigger Assessment Exercise: Create a Trigger Journal

Column 1: Specific Workplace Scenario.
Column 2: Emotional Response.
Column 3: Childhood Connection.
Column 4: Healing Strategy.

Example:

Scenario: Performance Review.

Emotional Response: Intense anxiety, feeling like a failure.

Childhood Connection: Critical parent, never feeling good enough.

Healing Strategy: Breathwork, positive self-talk, recognising review as professional feedback, not personal judgment.

Boundary-Setting Toolkit

Practical Boundary Scripts:

'I appreciate the opportunity, but my current workload doesn't allow me to take this on.'
'I need some time to consider this request.'
'I'm happy to discuss this during work hours.'

Boundary-Setting Practice:

Identify your current boundary challenges.
Write out specific scenarios.
Develop clear, kind response scripts.
Practice with a trusted friend.

Emotional Regulation Techniques for Professional Settings

Grounding Techniques for Workplace Stress:

4-7-8 Breathing Method

Inhale for 4 counts.
Hold for 7 counts.
Exhale for 8 counts.

Repeat 4 times when feeling overwhelmed

Desk Meditation

2-minute mindfulness practice.
Focus on breath.
Release tension in shoulders.
Remind yourself: 'I am safe. I am capable.'

Reframing Professional Self-Worth – Limiting Belief Transformation Exercise:

Old Belief: 'I'm not good enough'.

Evidence Gathering:

List 5 professional achievements.
Note the skills you've developed.
Recognise challenges you've overcome.

Reframed Belief: 'I am continuously learning and growing.'

Navigating Difficult Workplace Relationships - Communication Strategy:

Identify the underlying emotion.
Use 'I' statements.
Stay professional and calm.
Know when to seek additional support.

Example:

'I feel concerned about our communication approach. I want to discuss how we can work more effectively together.'

Imposter Syndrome Management

Having imposter syndrome means that you never feel 'good enough.' Challenge these thoughts. Where is the evidence that you are not good enough?

Try these confidence-building practices:

Create a 'Success Portfolio' - this will become your 'evidence' that you are good enough! And every time you feel that the imposter syndrome feeling's coming back, just read through this folder. All the success that you put into it will force you to challenge your thoughts.

Document professional wins.
Save positive feedback.
Track personal growth.

Daily Affirmation Practice

'My worth is not determined by external validation.'
'I bring unique value to my workplace.'
'I am learning and growing every day'.

Recognising And Addressing Workplace Trauma

Red Flags:

Consistent anxiety about work.
Physical symptoms (headaches, stomach issues).
Feeling constantly on edge.
Difficulty sleeping.
Excessive people-pleasing.

Support Strategies:

Consider trauma-informed therapy.
Explore employee assistance programs.
Build a support network.
Practice radical self-care.

Your Professional Healing Journey

Your professional life is not a battlefield to survive but a landscape to explore, grow, and thrive in. The resilience that helped you survive childhood will help you create a career that honors your whole self. Every boundary you set, every trigger you understand, every moment of self-compassion is a step toward professional healing.

Key Takeaways From Chapter 8: Professional Life and Inner Child Healing

What We Have Learned

Understanding Your Professional Self
Workplace behaviors are deeply connected to childhood experiences.
Survival skills learned in childhood directly impact professional interactions.
Your worth is not determined by productivity.

Recognising Workplace Survival Patterns

People-pleasing as a protective mechanism.
Overworking to prove value.
Difficulty setting boundaries.
Imposter syndrome roots.
Fear of failure or criticism.

Core Healing Strategies

Develop emotional intelligence.
Create intentional professional boundaries.
Transform survival skills into strengths.
Practice compassionate self-awareness.
Interrupt old emotional patterns.

Essential Healing Tools

Trigger mapping in workplace scenarios

Emotional regulation practices.
Authentic communication strategies.
Confidence-building exercises.
Self-worth validation techniques.

Rebuilding Professional Confidence

Childhood experiences are not limitations.
Professional growth is a healing journey.
Your unique experiences are strengths.

Practical Action Steps

Create a professional trigger journal.
Develop boundary-setting scripts.
Practice workplace meditation.
Build a supportive network.
Seek trauma-informed support.

Chapter 9: Your Healing Journey - Moving Forward with Courage and Hope

The Transformation You Have Begun

You've traveled a remarkable path through this book; be proud of yourself! —from understanding the wounds of your inner child to developing tools of healing, compassion, and self-discovery. Healing is personal growth. As you reach this final chapter, take a moment to recognise the incredible courage it has taken to explore the deepest parts of your inner landscape—to confront the wounds that have shaped your life and to choose a different way of being. Healing is rarely a straightforward path. It's an intricate journey of discovery and compassion.

This book contains many exercises that you could incorporate into a personal toolkit to continue your healing journey. It is there for you to personalise—make it your own and fit what you need.

You HAVE A RIGHT TO BE HAPPY!

The tools you've learned are not just techniques—they're bridges to a more authentic self. Emotional mapping helps you understand the language of your body, journaling provides a safe space for expression, and self-compassion practices have become your gentle revolution against years of self-criticism.

Your Journey in Perspective

Think back to where you started:

Carrying unresolved childhood pain.
Struggling with emotional triggers.
Feeling disconnected from yourself.
Believing your past defines your future.

Now, you've learned that:

Your wounds do not determine your worth.
Healing is a courageous, ongoing process.
You have the power to rewrite your story.
Compassion begins with how you treat yourself.

The Healing Toolkit You've Developed

Reflect on the key tools you've learned:

Emotional Mapping

Understanding where emotions live in your body.
Recognising triggers and patterns.
Creating space for emotional exploration.

Journaling as Transformation

Releasing guilt and shame.
Continuous and non-linear.
Rewriting your personal narrative.
Connecting with your inner child.

Self-Compassion Practices

Gentle self-talk
Meditation and visualisation
Setting healthy boundaries

This book has taught you to have key mindset shifts,

understanding survival to thrive
From people pleasing to authentic engagement

From fear of failure to embracing growth
From external validation to internal worth

Continuing Your Healing Journey: Focused Resources

Recommended Reading List

'Complex PTSD: From Surviving to Thriving'' - Pete Walker
'The Body Keeps the Score' - Bessel van der Kolk
Adult Children of Emotionally Immature Parents' - Lindsay Gibson
Self-Compassion' - Kristin Neff

Key Takeaways from Each:

Walker: Understanding survival mechanisms
Van der Kolk: Body-based trauma healing
Gibson: Recognizing childhood emotional patterns
Neff: Developing self-compassion techniques

Online Resources

- Free Healing Platforms:
- CPTSD Foundation website
- Reddit r/CPTSDHealing community
- Trauma recovery podcasts
- YouTube healing channels

Personal Healing Toolkit – Essential Toolkit Items:

Dedicated healing journal
Comfort objects
Meditation app
Stress relief tools
Affirmation Cards (I have put together a set of digital affirmation cards that you can download for free – click on the QR code at the front of the book)
Emotional regulation worksheets
This book

Toolkit Purpose:

Create a safe healing environment
Provide consistent support
Track personal growth
Offer immediate comfort

Practical Healing Practices:

Monthly Commitment Plan
Weekly journaling
Daily 10-minute meditation
Monthly personal healing review
Practice Goals
Consistent self-care
Regular emotional check-ins
Structured healing approach
Measurable personal development

A Powerful Closing Exercise: Writing Your Future

Take out your journal and complete this guided reflection:

Part 1: Acknowledge Your Journey

List three significant insights you've gained
Recognise the strength it took to begin this healing process
Celebrate the courage of your inner child

Part 2: Envision Your Future Self

Write a letter to yourself five years from now:
Describe the emotional freedom you've achieved
Detail the relationships you've healed
Paint a picture of the peace you've discovered

Part 3: Commit to Continuous Growth

Create a personal manifesto of healing:

I promise to be gentle with myself
I choose compassion over criticism
My past does not define my future

I am worthy of love and healing

Part 4: Navigating Setbacks with Grace

Remember: Healing is not linear. There will be days when:

Old patterns feel comfortable
Triggers catch you off guard
Progress seems slow

Part 5: Your new tools will help you:

Pause and breathe
Practice self-compassion
Return to your healing practices
Treat yourself with kindness

Daily Practices for Ongoing Healing

Morning Ritual

- 5-minute meditation
- Gentle body scan
- Affirmation: 'I am safe. I am loved. I am healing.'

Evening Reflection

- Gratitude journaling
- Emotional mapping
- Compassionate self-check-in

When to Seek Additional Support

It's okay to need help. Consider:

- Trauma-informed therapy
- Support groups
- Healing workshops
- Trusted friends or mentors

A Final Message to Your Inner Child

Close your eyes. Imagine yourself at the age when you first felt wounded. Place your hand on your heart and speak these words:

'I SEE YOU. I HEAR YOU. YOU ARE BRAVE. YOU ARE LOVED. YOU ARE SAFE NOW. WE ARE HEALING TOGETHER.'

The Continuous Journey

One of the most powerful practices in healing is the ability to envision a future beyond your past pain. This isn't about toxic positivity or dismissing your experiences. Instead, it's about recognising that you are not defined by what happened to you but by your incredible capacity for resilience, love, and transformation. Healing is not a destination—it's a lifelong journey of:

Self-discovery
Compassion
Growth
Love

You are not alone. Every step you take is an act of courage. This book ends, but your healing continues. Embrace each moment with the following:

Curiosity
Compassion

As you close this book, understand that you're not closing a chapter but opening a new way of being. Your healing is an ongoing commitment—to yourself, the child within you, and the incredible potential of your life. You are not broken. You are not defined by your past. You are a remarkable human, capable of extraordinary healing and growth.

I would like to take this final opportunity to thank you for buying this book. I truly hope that you have gained a lot of knowledge that you will use in your healing journey.

Remember: Healing is not about perfection. It's about progress. It's about showing up for yourself again and again.

You are not your past.

You are not your wounds

You are possibility.

You are resilience.

You are love.

Keep going.

Keep healing.

Keep becoming.

You have everything you need within you.

· ♥ · ♥ · ♥ · ♥ · ♥ ·

Keeping the Journey Alive

Now that you have everything you need to reconnect with your inner child and start your healing journey, it's time to pass that knowledge forward.

By leaving an honest review of this book on Amazon, you'll help other readers find the same guidance and support you've discovered. Your words could be the encouragement someone else needs to take that first brave step toward healing – please use the QR code to leave your review.

Thank you for being part of this mission. The journey of self-discovery and healing continues when we share what we've learned—and you're helping to make that possible.

• ♥ • ♥ • ♥ • ♥ • ♥ •

References

Goodenough, E. (n.d.). *Children never forget*. University of Michigan. Retrieved from https://sites.lsa.umich.edu/elizabethgoodenough/wp-content/uploads/sites/206/2014/12/Goodenough_Children-Never-Forget.pdf

Karantzas, G. C., McCabe, M. P., & Allen, N. B. (2021). *Childhood emotional maltreatment and romantic relationships in adulthood: A systematic review and meta-analysis. Frontiers in Psychology, 12*, 8666543. https://pmc.ncbi.nlm.nih.gov/articles/PMC8666543/

PsychCentral. (n.d.). *Neuroplasticity and childhood trauma: Effects, healing, and recovery*. Retrieved from https://psychcentral.com/ptsd/the-roles-neuroplasticity-and-emdr-play-in-healing-from-childhood-trauma

Ackerman, C. E. (n.d.). *21 mindfulness exercises & activities for adults (+ PDF)*. Positive Psychology. Retrieved from https://positivepsychology.com/mindfulness-exercises-techniques-activities/

Mayo Clinic. (n.d.). *Resilience: Build skills to endure hardship*. Retrieved from https://www.mayoclinic.org/tests-procedures/resilience-training/in-depth/resilience/art-20046311

American Psychological Association. (n.d.). *Mindfulness meditation: A research-proven way to reduce stress*. Retrieved from https://www.apa.org/topics/mindfulness/meditation

Healthline. (n.d.). *30 grounding techniques to quiet distressing thoughts*. Retrieved from https://www.healthline.com/health/grounding-techniques

New Hope Mental Health Center. (n.d.). *Harnessing the power of visualization: How imagery can transform mental health*. Retrieved from https://www.thenewhopemhcs.com/harnessing-the-power-of-visualization/

WebMD. (n.d.). *Mental health benefits of journaling*. Retrieved from https://www.webmd.com/mental-health/mental-health-benefits-of-journaling

Kids First Services. (n.d.). *Top art therapy techniques to heal from trauma*. Retrieved from https://www.kidsfirstservices.com/first-insights/art-therapy-techniques-for-processing-trauma

Quenza. (n.d.). *Empowering emotional growth: Effective psychological assessment tools for emotional intelligence*. Retrieved from https://quenza.com/blog/knowledge-base/psychological-assessment-tools-for-emotional-intelligence/

BetterHelp. (n.d.). *Healing through storytelling: How stories can help you process trauma*. Retrieved from https://www.betterhelp.com/advice/research/healing-through-storytelling-how-narratives-can-help-you-process-trauma/

Lion's Roar. (n.d.). *A meditation to heal your inner child*. Retrieved from https://www.lionsroar.com/heal-your-inner-child-meditation/

Ackerman, C. E. (n.d.). *8 powerful self-compassion exercises & worksheets*. Positive Psychology. Retrieved from https://positivepsychology.com/self-compassion-exercises-worksheets/

Bajaj, K. (n.d.). *4-7-8 relaxing breath*. Retrieved from https://www.kerrybajaj.com/blog/4-7-8-relaxing-breath

Inner Serenity. (n.d.). *Affirmations for shame*. Retrieved from https://innerserenity.world/affirmations-for-shame/

Right Home Remedies. (n.d.). *Mastering mindfulness: Daily practices for mental health*. Retrieved from https://righthomeremedies.com/daily-practices-for-mental-health/

Listly. (n.d.). *10 simple ways to meditate*. Retrieved from https://list.ly/list/eDV-10-simple-ways-to-meditate

Printed in Great Britain
by Amazon